HOLLAND COOKERY

For Pat and Jane Finn ~
with warmest wishes for
happy cooking !

Mieke Michael ♪♫

♡ February 14, 2002

Illustrated by
Felicia Michael

THIRD PRINTING

HOLLAND COOKERY
by
Mieke

Printed by Rapid Repro of Danbury, CT

This Bi-centennial symbol represents
over 200 years of unbroken friendship between
The Netherlands and The United States

Manufactured in the United States of America
ISBN 0-9609304-0-X
Revised, Enlarged and Reprinted   1994

FOR

Claudia

Eric

Marika

Emily

James

CONTENTS

ABOUT HOLLAND -- THE LAND AND THE PEOPLE

Holland is the name given to the kingdom of the Netherlands, a small nation whose imperial reach and affinity to the sea have shaped its history and culture, and definitely influenced its cuisine.

Half its people dwell below the level of the sea, because for almost ten centuries the Dutch have been creating their land -- stealing it from the sea and lakes and marshes.

It is the land of tulips, dikes and wooden shoes. Wide canals wind through green lowlands; farms and pastures stretch for miles without a hill. Windmills, their giant cloth sails picking up every breeze, guard the lowland reclaimed from the sea. These polders are protected from inundation by dunes and dikes. The Dutch have had to build many dams to keep the rivers and canals in their course, and this is why so many Dutch cities end in "dam."

The traditional dress is different in every province, but is fast disappearing in younger generations. The people in the farmlands and fishing villages still wear klompen (wooden shoes). Each village that clings to its past has its own traditional costume. Those in the know can not only tell where a woman lives by her clothing, but whether she is a Catholic or Protestant, married or single.

The land is compact and planned, much of it wrested as it was from the sea. As a result, the people are a reflection of their history and their environment.

Churches, castles and strongholds dating back as far as the seventh century still exist in Holland.

Houses are brick, windows sparkling and giving full views of neat shining interiors, all proudly displaying an array of colorful Delft, glowing pewter and polished brass. Even the sidewalls are spotless, and flowers grow on every foot of available soil, around doorways and in brightly painted window-boxes.

The Dutch were pioneers in diamond cutting, pottery and fine earthenware (Delft since 1653, Makkumware since 1660), printing, bulb growing, dairy farming, and cheese making. Artists and sculptors hail from Holland and are represented in museums throughout the world. In addition, Hugo Grotius founded the study of international law, Anton van Leeuwenhoek invented the microscope, and Christian Huygens originated the pendulum clock.

Some other brief and interesting facts which got the world in Dutch: as the first settlers of New York, then called Nieuw Amsterdam, the Dutch brought the first governor (Pieter Stuyvesant), the first clergyman, the first mayor, and the first teacher to these shores -- even the tradition of Santa Claus as Saint Nicholas! And every schoolchild knows that Pieter Minuit purchased Manhattan Island from the Indians for a mere 24 dollars worth of trinkets, surely the most memorable real estate transaction in history!

Because the land is so small (120 by 190 miles and less than 16,000 square miles total), the boundaries touch several other countries, and as a result the Dutch people have a flair for other languages which by necessity are taught early in grade schools. They possess a wry sense of humor, innate stubbornness born of determination, and appreciation of good hearty food. Courtesy and politeness are universal traits -- the same extreme friendliness and cordiality are extended whether one purchases a painting or a postage stamp.

The gateway to Europe is truly through the Dutch Door!

ABOUT HOLLAND COOKERY

Dutch gastronomy is rather like the Dutch people themselves: hearty, strong and real. There is considerable diversity and international flavor in menus and cooking terms, owing to the small size of the land itself, whose boundaries touch Belgium, France and Germany. Then too there is another significant tangent—the exotic fare influenced strongly by past association with the East Indies and the consequent Indonesian heritage of a sprinkling of Netherlanders.

The Dutch are not a nation of calorie-counters, a fact which is much appreciated by the visitor and applauded by themselves. They have ingeniously adapted their own resourcefulness to the gastronomic bests of their neighbors: egg and pastry cooking of Belgium, mushroom-wine tastes of France, onion-vinegar touches of Germany, exotic spicing and pungent combinations from the Indies. Thus the culinary art of the Netherlands emerges as an ambience of heritage, customs and geography.

Strictly native are the proud and varied collection of soups, baked goods, and hearty winter-casserole fare. And importantly, there are zesty methods of preparing meats, cheese and fish dishes, sauces and desserts in which Dutch cooks take second place to none in the world.

In this volume, I have tried to assemble the foods, anecdotes and related information with which I have been so familiar since childhood, when my parents came to U.S. shores from the Netherlands Royal Opera as Victor recording artists. Included, besides translations from well-worn Holland cookbooks, are recipes and preparation methods from both their towns of Tilburg and Zwolle, and the grandparental ones of Breda, Arnhem, Utrecht and Deventer. In addition, many friends of Dutch extraction have allowed me the use of their inherited favorites, rounding out a diverse collection from most of the ten provinces, each with endemic peculiarities of food customs and preparation methods.

The end result, hopefully, is a compact volume, encompassing as it does the perennial favorites, national flavor and the best of Holland-to-the-core cookery.

APPETIZERS
(VOORSPYSEN)

The appetizer, or *voorspys* literally translated, means "pre-meal" and is served as a separate course hot or cold, with accompanying cutlery and appropriate wine to awaken the tastebuds and stimulate the palate. Unlike so-called cocktail nibbles and dips, it is not served as a rule in the pick-and-bite manner. The traditional late-evening drink, known affectionately as *borreltje*, may be offered together with spicy, cheesy or salty bits, and at festive gatherings might include several of the savories whose recipes I have listed in this chapter.

Bitterballetjes	Oesters Margriet
Lever Pastei	Haring met uitjes
Gerookte paling	Garnalen champignons
Kaas stokjes	Gember met kaas

BITTERBALLETJES
(BITTER BALLS)
This is the most widely served hot appetizer in Holland. Put any leftover meat (or cooked soup-shank meat) through the coarse food chopper. You should have about 2 cups meat. Make thick ragôut sauce with:

2 tbsps. margarine
½ cup flour
1 tbsp. salt
1 cup milk or soup stock
¼ tsp. paprika
¼ tsp. pepper
1 rounded tbsp. chopped parsley (fresh!)
1 tsp- Worcestershire Sauce
1 chopped onion
½ tsp. curry powder
soup plate of bread crumbs for dipping
2-3 beaten raw eggs in small bowl

Make white sauce of melted butter, flour and milk in good-sized saucepan. When smooth, add seasonings and parsley. Add meat. Spread on large flat meat platter to cool. Roll mixture into small balls (about an inch in diameter) in floured hands. Roll in beaten raw eggs and then in crumbs. Set aside to firm. (May be made a day ahead.) Now fry in hot fat until golden brown. Serve piping hot with toothpicks and pass a hot mustard alongside. Make plenty!

LEVER PASTEI
(LIVER PATÉ)
My father's brother was the pastor of a small farm parish in Azewyn, province of Gelderland. He used goose liver for this favorite recipe of his, but fresh chicken livers do just fine.

Brown gently ½ stick (4 tbsps. margarine or butter. Add: 1 lb. chicken livers and sauté Next, stir in: juice of 1 lemon   2 tbsps. onion juice or
    1 large grated onion ½ tsp. salt and a good   ¼ cup mayonnaise
    bit of fresh pepper

Remove from heat when livers are browned but still soft. Mash right in the skillet with coarse potato masher or put through coarse sieve when slightly cooled. In a bowl, mash 2 hard-boiled eggs and add liver mixture. Mix well with ¼ cup mayonnaise and lastly add 3 tbsp. dry sherry. Garnish with parsley after turning it onto a large round plate. May be served on toast rounds or as a spread with a small butter knife. Tastier when made a day ahead and even freezes well.

GEROOKTE PALING
(SMOKED EEL)
Smoked eel is obtainable in many gourmet delicatessens and near any salty shore. This is a great favorite with the men and for those not figure-conscious.

       1 or 2 smoked eels (the plumper the better)
       lemon wedges
       parsley, chopped fine
Eel is skinned easily when cut into 2-inch wedges with a sharp knife. Discard the head and tail sections. Pass toothpicks or cocktail forks. Another thing—be sure to scrape the succulent inside of the smoked skin. As children, my brothers and I always thought this was the best part.

KAAS STOKJES
(HOT CHEESE STICKS)
3 cups grated or shredded cheese
(Cheddar, Edam or Gouda are good.)
1 tsp. salt
¼ tsp. pepper
2 cups sifted flour
1 stick margarine or butter (soft)
4 tbsps. milk
Sift together the flour and salt and pepper, add butter and cheese. Blend with fork until crumbly, then stir in milk. Mixture should be moist. On slightly floured board, roll with palm of hand or rolling pin until you have a flat sheet about ¾ inch thick. With sharp knife, cut sticks in 3-inch lengths.

Bake at 375 degrees about 10-12 minutes. This will make about 6 dozen sticks. Serve them hot and pass plenty of napkins as they should be eaten with the fingers. Be sure to grease the cookie sheet!

OESTERS MARGRIET
(OYSTERS MARGUERITE)
1 qt. oysters
Blanch and chop very fine.
1 tbsp. Hollandaise sauce
Mix with the oysters. Spread on pieces of toast.
dash Worcestershire
3 tbsps. chopped parsley
salt to taste
Sprinkle on top of each round of toast and put in 350 degrees F. oven for 3 minutes. 1 tsp. butter for each piece of toast. Serve hot. Serves 8.

HARING MET UITJES
(SPICED FRESH HERRING)
There is nothing more delectable than herring eaten fresh (we call it green) at the stands in Amsterdam. But this is surely second best.

Use fresh herring, or salted herring soaked overnight. Put 4-5 herrings in bowl after cutting in small pieces. Add ½ cup vinegar or white wine, 1 tbsp. brown sugar, and a heaping cup of thinly sliced onions. Add a few whole cloves and peppercorns. Cover. Keep in refrigerator about 1 week until bones soften. Serve with toothpicks and watch them disappear.

GARNALEN CHAMPIGNONS
(SHRIMP-STUFFED MUSHROOMS)
In the Netherlands as in most of Europe, the shrimp are tiny and sweet, comparable to our Gulf variety. Larger shrimp must be chopped fine.

15

12 large white firm mushrooms
3 tbsps. butter or margarine
1 small onion, minced
1 cup breadcrumbs (packaged ones are fine)
½ cup cooked shrimp, chopped
½ tsp. oregano or marjoram
2-3 tbsps. sherry

Carefully remove stems from washed and wiped mushrooms, chop stems fine. In a skillet or shallow saucepan, heat 1 tbsp. of the butter, add the onion and the chopped stems, cook about 2 minutes, stirring. Add crumbs, shrimp and sherry, remove from heat. Add seasonings. Preheat broiler. On a large baking sheet, place mushroom caps, inverted, and brush with the remaining butter, melted. Broil about 2 minutes. Remove from broiler, turn up again and fill with shrimp mixuture. Dot with a piece of butter on each and broil for another 3-4 minutes until bubbling hot. Serve with plenty of cocktail napkins on large toothpicks. These sound complicated but are simple and delicious. Yield: 12 hors d'oeuvres.

GEMBER MET KAAS
(GINGER-CHEESE CANAPÉ)

1 cup (1 pkg.) ginger pieces 2 cups diced pieces Edam or Gouda cheese

On toothpicks, put a piece of cheese, then ginger, then cheese. (3 in all per toothpick.) These are equally great with cold beer or cocktails and are frequently served late at night with a *borreltje* (nightcap).

SOUPS
(SOEPEN)

Few menu standbys are as essential a part of the Dutch cook's repertoire as are the wide variety of soups. Accordingly, there are savory extracts of practically every meat, vegetable and marrow-bone. Even for routine meals, Dutch dinner tables often boast cream soups smooth and delicate, clear soups without a trace of scum, or soups so thick that a spoon or ladle has a solid stand in the pot. Many a winter repast might consist solely of one of these hearty offerings, together with rich dark bread and a pudding dessert, and most Hollanders have come to feel that it just isn't a robust meal without a prelude of their favorite. A true representation of all the specials both standard and traditional would be a tome in itself, but I have included what are considered generally to be the best examples:

Erwtensoep
Echte groentensoep
Amandelsoep
Tomatensoep met bal-
   letjes
Koolsoep
Preisoep *bonne*
   femme
Wortelsoep

Champignonsoep
Amsterdamse soepketel
Knolselderysoep
Aardappelsoep
Bloemkoolsoep
Zuurkoolsoep
Kaas en groentensoep
Koninginnensoep

ERWTENSOEP (SNERT)
TRADITIONAL DUTCH PEA SOUP
FROM MY FATHER'S HOME TOWN.

Recipe from Zwolle (in the province of Overysel.)

Large pork knuckle or hambone
½ lb. fresh (not smoked) bacon
1 lb. pkg. green split peas (soak for 1 hr.)
1 bunch green celery, including leaves
1 root celery (if obtainable)
2-3 thick leeks (a *must*)
1 lb. smoked sausage (optional)

Place knuckle or hambone and the bacon in a large kettle with cold water to cover. Simmer for 2-2½ hours. Skim. Add peas, celery, leeks. Cook for another hour or until vegetables are tender. Add more boiling water if necessary. Add sausage, sliced, for last 20 minutes of cooking. Salt and pepper to taste. Serve with crusty rye or pumpernickel. Cannot possibly be overcooked and tastes even better after third day of reheating. Do not burn!

ECHTE GROENTEN SOEP
(REAL DUTCH VEGETABLE SOUP)
(from Noord Brabant)

Most Dutch Sunday dinners start with a soup. In any season and in all provinces, this is the favorite.

> 1 large beef shank (with lots of meat on it)
> 4 qts. cold water
> 1 tsp. salt (add more later if desired)
> 1 cup chopped celery
> 3 good-sized carrots, chopped
> 6 beef bouillon cubes
> 1 small can tomatoes (optional)

Starting with cold water, bring shank to a boil and turn heat to low. Let simmer, covered, for 1½ hours; skim. Now add celery and carrots, cook ½ to ¾ hour longer. Tomatoes may be added 5 minutes before serving. Add bouillon cubes and stir. The soupmeat is usually served on side dishes with mustard and horseradish and a piccalilli relish. See Ragout Croquetten for a delicious leftover soup-meat recipe.

Note: The Dutch always keep a bottle of Maggi liquid seasoning on the table in a handsome silver server, to add extra flavor for those wishing it.

TOMATEN SOEP MET BALLETJES
(TOMATO SOUP WITH CURRY BALLS)
(Mieke's own recipe)

> 2 qts. beef broth or stock
> 8 large tomatoes, scalded, peeled and chopped
> 1 bay leaf
> 1 lb. beef or veal, ground (½ pork may be used
>   for added flavor)
> 1 egg
> ½ cup bread crumbs
> ¼ tsp. curry powder
> salt and pepper to taste
> 1 thinly sliced onion
> pre-cooked rice, (optional)

Simmer the tomatoes in the stock with bay leaf and seasoning for 1 hour. Meanwhile, mix meatball mixture and shape into balls about an inch in diameter. Set balls aside to chill and firm. Then drop one by one into soup and let simmer all together one hour longer. Add rice, if desired, 10 minutes before serving, but keep stirring. May be garnished with parsley or fresh dill, even a glob of whipped cream if you feel flush.

AMANDEL SOEP
(CREAM OF ALMOND SOUP)
(from Utrecht)

1 cup whole blanched almonds	1 cup milk
2 tbsps. butter or margarine	1 cup light cream
2 tbsps. flour	salt
3 cups chicken stock	white pepper
	pinch of mace

Grate the almonds, or whirl in electric blender. Melt butter in large saucepan. Blend in flour. Add chicken stock gradually. (Use water and chicken bouillon cubes if you don't have stock.) Bring to a boil. Add grated almonds and simmer about 10 minutes. Add milk and cream. Season to taste with salt and pepper; add mace. Heat through, but do not boil. Makes about 5 cups.

WITTEKOOLSOEP
(CABBAGE SOUP WITH PORK)

2 tsps. butter or margarine
¼ lb. lean salt pork or country-style bacon, diced
¼ large cabbage (or ½ small), coarsely sliced
  (ribs out)
2 tbsps. flour
3 qts. water
¼ tsp. each salt, pepper, nutmeg, cinammon
1 cup heavy cream
2 egg yolks

In a large saucepan melt butter, add pork, and brown. Add cabbage and onion, cook for a few minutes. Sprinkle in flour, blend with huge wooden spoon. Stirring, add 3 qts. water and spices. Bring to boil, simmer 1½ hours. In soup tureen, pour in cream which has been beaten with the egg yolks. Stirring, gradually add hot soup. Toasted French bread may be floated on top. Serves 8.

This recipe was given to me by a farmer's wife in the province of Gelderland. She claims it is even better when heated the second day.

PREISOEP BONNE FEMME
(BELGIAN LEEK SOUP)

4 tbsps. butter or margarine
freshly ground pepper
1 large bunch fresh leeks
2 medium boiling potatoes
2 qts. beef stock or 2 qts. water and 6 bouillon
    cubes
4 ribs celery and 2 sprigs parsley, tied together

This potato soup is another borrow from the Southern provinces, hence the French name. I have tasted and tried three different ways to make it, and this is not only easiest but everybody's favorite.

Bring water to a boil, adding bouillon cubes crumbled, and the celery-parsley bouquet. (If you are starting from scratch with a shank bone and water, boil gently for 1½ hours to make stock.)

Discard outer edges of leeks and cut off bad ends. Wash leeks thoroughly. Cut them into ½-inch slices, using all of green part if not too tough. In large skillet, sauté leek slices in the margarine for about 5 minutes, stirring. Cut in the potatoes, diced. Add 3 cups water and when it boils, turn down heat and simmer until potato-leek mix is tender, about 25 minutes. Take potato masher or large fork and make mix as fine as possible. Meantime, remove bouquet from stock. Add the leek mixture and simmer the entire soup for another half-hour. Pass a toasted, buttered rye bread and serve the soup in a tureen—it deserves it.

PEEN SOEP
(CARROT SOUP)
(from Noord Brabant)

4 tbsps. butter
6 carrots, sliced
1 cup sliced celery root (optional)
2 sliced onions

21

2 qts. stock or 1 qt. water w/6 bouillon cubes
3 tbsps. farina
½ tsp. pepper
dash of nutmeg
2 tbsps. chopped parsley

Melt the butter in a saucepan. Add the carrots, onion, and celery root. Sauté for 15 minutes, stirring frequently. Add to the stock and stir. Cover and cook over low heat for 45 minutes. Force the soup and vegetables through a fine sieve or place in an electric blender. Return the soup to the saucepan. Add the farina, pepper, and nutmeg, stirring constantly. Cook over low heat for 20 minutes. Correct seasoning. Sprinkle parsley on each portion before serving. Serve with crusty pumpernickel.

CHAMPIGNON SOEP
(DUTCH MUSHROOM SOUP)
(from Brabant)

1 lb. mushrooms	8 cups water
1 small onion	2 tsps. salt
8 tbsps. butter	8 tbsps. flour
2 cups rich milk	1 cup cream
few grains cayenne	½ tsp. pepper
paprika	

Save out a few of the mushroom caps to add to soup. Cover mushroom caps and stems, which have been peeled and chopped, with water. Add sliced onion and salt and boil slowly for about one-half hour. Melt butter in top of double boiler and add the mushroom caps which have been chopped. Cook about 3 minutes over flame. Add flour and milk to make a smooth thick sauce.

Add mushroom liquor and mushrooms rubbed through a sieve. Add cayenne, pepper, paprika and cream just before serving. Serves 10-12.

OVER 1,000 MILLS...

and each one different !

ART &
ANTIQUES

CLOCKS
OLD DOLLS
CHURCH FIGURES
COFFEE URNS
CARVED CHESTS
CHAIRS
WOOD CARVINGS
MOLDS, stained glass
ART WORKS

ANSTERDAMSE SOEPKETEL
(AMSTERDAM CHICKEN CHOWDER)
(This is my own name for a recipe given to me years ago in a pension off the Kalverstraat.)

1 leftover chicken, or most of it	2 tbsp. butter or margarine
2 tbsps. flour	1 huge onion, diced
1 qt. milk (4 cups)	3-4 strips lean bacon, cut up
3 boiled potatoes, diced	parsley or chives for garnish

Clean chicken of all meat and simmer cut-up carcass in 2 cups water for about 30 minutes. Any leftover gravy may be added if you have it. Remove bones and discard. Add the diced cold chicken and simmer another few minutes. Remove from heat and add the milk. In shallow saucepan or skillet, sauté the bacon pieces, onion, and potatoes. When golden, add butter and flour, simmer few minutes. Add milk and chicken mixture to this, stir gently. Heat through but do not boil. Add freshly ground pepper and garnish with chopped parsley or chives. Serves 6.

AARDAPPEL SOEP
(POTATO SOUP)
(Friesland)

6 medium-sized potatoes	4 tbsps. flour
2 qts. milk	3 tsps. salt
4 onions	2 stalks celery, chopped
6 tbsps. butter	dash cayenne pepper
	2 tsps. minced parsley

Slice potatoes and cook in boiling water until tender, scald milk in double boiler with onion and celery, remove, mix butter and flour, add to above. Add seasoning, sprinkle with parsley and serve hot. Serves 8-10.

KNOLSELDERIJ SOEP
(KNOB CELERY SOUP)

3 large knobs celery
2 qts. water
nutmeg (fresh grated), salt, pepper, and lemon
 juice to taste
a cupful of roux made from butter, flour, and
 milk

Peel the celery and cut in strips, cook until tender in the water and salt. Strain celery into colander, reserve liquid. Make the roux and add soup liquid gradually to it. Let boil through, add ½ cup more butter or margarine, then nutmeg and a bit of fresh lemon juice. Add celery strips last and stir carefully. More nutmeg may be sprinkled on top of individual bowl servings. Delicious winter fare!

BLOEMKOOL SOEP
(CAULIFLOWER-BUTTERMILK SOUP)

1 large head cauliflower, cut in thin slices
3 cups water
1 cup sliced onion (scallions are good too)
3 green peppers, slivered
2 cups light or medium cream
1 cup buttermilk
2 tsps. salt
¼ tsp. pepper
½ tsp. curry powder
¼ cup chopped parsley for garnish

In a good-sized soup pot, put the water, green pepper, onion and cauliflower. Bring to a rolling boil, turn to simmer and cover. Cook about 10-15 minutes until vegetables are fork-tender. Pour into a blender and whir at low speed, or put mixture through a coarse sieve. Pour smooth mixture back into the pot and add the cream, the buttermilk and the seasonings. Heat through without boiling, or chill thoroughly for a delicious summer luncheon soup. Garnish with parsley at serving time. Will fill 6 cream-soup bowls.

Note: This is an adaptation of a meatless Friday soup which was served regularly in a Gelderland Pensionnat where I attended school for a year. In the U.S. it would be equally delicious using broccoli as a variation instead of cauliflower.

ZUURKOOLSOEP
(SAUERKRAUT SOUP)

Sauerkraut is a winter staple, often kept in large barrels in the farm areas. When I lived in Gelderland for the greater part of a year, I used to enjoy watching the cabbages sliced and salted down. Many Saturdays this soup was standard fare in my uncle's household.

2 good-sized onions, sliced
Butter or margarine for browning
1 tbsp. tomato puree (optional, for color)
1½ lbs. (or large can) sauerkraut
2 qts. (8 cups) bouillon or meat stock

Melt butter in large soup kettle, add onion and brown. Using wooden spoon, stir in flour and tomato purée. Add sauerkraut, cover and simmer for a few minutes. Stir in the beef bouillon and cook over low heat for about 2 hours.

The cooked side meat from the stock may be served on the side, with a hearty mustard and pumpernickel bread. Makes 6 hearty bowls.

KAAS-GROENTEN SOEP
(CHEESE SOUP WITH VEGETABLES)

2 celery stalks (no leaves)
2 carrots
2 small onions
1 green pepper
3 cups grated cheese (Cheddar or Gouda)
5 tbsps. flour
1 qt. (4 cups) beef or chicken broth
2 cups milk
2 tbsps. dry sherry (optional)
salt and pepper to taste

Chop the 4 vegetables and cook in butter until tender. Stir in flour and slowly add broth, stirring constantly. Soup will thicken, so do not burn it. Gradually add cheese until melted, then milk and sherry. Remove from high heat and simmer very gently until heated but not boiling. May be served with a glob of whipped cream floating atop each bowl, and sprinkled with chopped parsley or chives. Will serve 6 to 8 depending on appetites or calorie-watching.

KONINGINNENSOEP
(QUEEN'S CHICKEN SOUP)
(from The Hague)

2½-3 qts. chicken broth (drawn from soup-chicken)
4 beaten egg yolks
½ cup light cream
¼ cup medium dry sherry
entire cooked chicken, diced
pinch curry or paprika
chopped parsley

Stir egg yolks, cream and sherry together in huge pot or tureen. Pour piping hot broth in slowly, stirring occasionally. Add diced chicken and sprinkle seasoning and parsley on top. Hurry the guests in and serve soup at once. Fit for the royal family, and you'll enjoy it just as much.

SALADS
(SLA GERECHTEN)

The Dutch word "sla" is the same for both lettuce and salad.

Dutch cuisine lays no great claims to salad recipes perhaps to the sparsity of salad-green varities or the reluctance of the homemaker to go wild over uncooked vegetables. Nor is lettuce used in the making of sandwiches! The Dutch will rather shun a crisp hard lettuce and search the market for "malse sla," meaning tender lettuce. Salads as a result tend to be prepared mixtures on beds of leaves, and not the dressing-tossed kind.

Kastanjesla
Knollensla
Komkommersla

Huzarensla
Heete Koolsla
Suiker-ei sla

KASTANJE SLA
(DUTCH STYLE CHESTNUT SALAD)
(from Azewyn, province of Gelderland)
First blanch one pt. of shelled chestnuts. Boil these in salted water until tender. Drain and cool. Then add an equal quantity of finely cut celery. Mix with mayonnaise and serve on leaves of lettuce.

KOMKOMMERSLA
(Town: Zwolle; Province, Overysel)

4 large cucumbers,	½ tsp. salt
fat and firm	4 tbsps. wine vinegar
freshly ground pepper	chopped chives (optional)
4 tbsps. salad oil	

Peel cucumbers, slice paper thin. In a large bowl, put the salt on them and mix. Now put a small plate or saucer directly on them, with a weight on it (canister, box of salt, or other heavy object to make a press). Let stand for at least 1 hour and then drain off the liquid. Cucumbers will now be limp and shapeless. Add oil-vinegar mix and toss well. Serve ice-cold, sprinkled with chives if desired. Delicious summer salad.

KNOLLENSLA
(TURNIP SALAD)
1 tbsp. lemon juice
¼ cup mayonnaise
½ cup raw turnip or rutabaga
1 cup shredded cabbage
1 cup red apples, unpeeled, but diced
¼ cup raisins
¼ cup chopped walnuts or pecans

Wash turnip, peel and grate. In bowl, combine lemon juice and mayonnaise. Mix remaining ingredients with wooden spoon. Chill entire mixture thoroughly and serve on Boston or Bibb lettuce. Additional dressing mix may be added on top if desired.

Iceberg lettuce is not traditionally used as a salad base in Holland. Even tossed salads are made with looser-leafed lettuce.

HUZARENSLA
There are many variations of this dish depending on location. This version comes from Heerlen, where I ate it first.)

Equal parts of:
>   salt herring (chopped)
>   diced beets
>   diced cooked cold potatoes
>   chopped sweet onions
>   chopped hardcooked eggs
>   diced sweet pickles (tiny gherkins may be used
>   whole)
>   freshly ground pepper

Marinate this mixture gently in dressing of 2 parts oil to 1 part wine vinegar. Serve icy-cold on bed of Boston (Bibb) lettuce and garnish with capers and/or wedges of lemon.

HEETE KOOL SLA
(COLE SLAW HOT)

1 large head cabbage	6 eggs
1 tsp. mustard	1 tsp. sugar
1 tsp. salt	½ cup vinegar
½ cup milk	cayenne to taste

Mix ingredients of sauce together and stir constantly to prevent curdling. When very hot remove from fire. As quickly as possible stir the raw sliced cabbage into sauce. Mix well.

DINA'S SUIKER-EI SLA
(Literally, this means "Sugar-Egg Salad"
and is an old farm-country standby.)
In a large bowl, slice paper-thin:

1 head lettuce
2 medium onions
now add juice of 2 lemons

Beat 2 raw eggs in separate bowl. Add 1 tbsp. sugar, some salt and pepper and dash of nutmeg. Mix all together. Serve ice-cold. This is an excellent complement to fish and is served regularly on Fridays in the Catholic South of Holland.

SIDE DISHES
(BYSCHOTELS)

If many food terms and recipes happen to end in the "je" or "ke" suffix, this is because it is the diminutive ending, widely used as the national idiom and a habitual standby in everyday conversation.

Side dishes, therefore, are often referred to as *warme hapjes*, or warm bites. Dutch side dishes consist often of leftover concoctions of egg, potato, and vegetable variations.

Every Holland family, whether average or affluent, knows how to turn yesterday's meal into *klikjes* of an entirely different nature flavorwise.

Some of these tempting dishes will suffice for a light supper, an auxiliary luncheon or a late-evening meal or perhaps even an accompaniment to the omnipresent Dutch *boterham* or elaborate sandwich meal. Most of those here listed, with the exception of the turnip soufflé,are traditional and have merit in their keeping and reheating qualities.

Slier asperges met ei
Aardappel balletjes
Gestoofde prei
Gelderland omelette
Zoetzuur roode kool
Witlof

Aardappel-kaas croquetten
Knollenpot
Knollensoufflé
Uitsmyter
Boeren omelette

SLIER ASPERGES MET EI
(ASPARAGUS DUTCH STYLE)
(In Holland, the asparagus are kept out of the sun and are snow-white. The most famous growing locale is Bergen-op-Zoom. People will not buy them unless they fairly crackle with freshness).

Wash asparagus, cut off coarse ends, and soak in cold salted water for an hour. Drain. Put in pot with fresh cold water (preferably in pressure cooker) and boil until tender. Meantime, hardboil 1-2 eggs per person and melt (not brown!) ¼ cup butter or margarine for each. Put hot asparagus lengthwise on platter and surround with the eggs (quartered) and pass melted butter. Each guest mashes his own egg on his plate, adds melted butter and dips in the asparagus, which are then eaten with the fingers and served as a traditional first course all through asparagus season. Delicious!

AARDAPPEL BALLETJES
(POTATO BALLS)
For every 4 cups leftover mashed potatoes, allow 2 eggs. Separate yolks and mix these with potatoes. Add ¼ tsp. nutmeg. Beat egg whites until stiff, fold gently into mixture. Form into 1-inch balls between palms of your hands. Roll in seasoned breadcrumbs and fry in deep hot fat until golden brown.

My maternal grandmother came from Breda and had this recipe in her bridal cookbook.

GESTOOFDE PREI
(STEWED OR BRAISED LEEKS)
In the Netherlands as in most of Europe, leek is considered to be a tasty vegetable and side dish, rather than just a soup additive as it is in the States.

2 good-sized bunches
  fresh leeks
freshly ground pep-
  per, salt to taste

½ cup butter or margarine
water to simmer

In large skillet, melt butter slowly. Have leeks washed thoroughly, as fresh leeks may have sand clinging to the inner leaves. Slice leeks in ½-inch pieces and wash them again. Put in skillet with the margarine and sauté gently, stirring with a wooden spoon. Add about a cup of water and continue cooking until leeks are tender. Season and serve hot. A small amount of cream was always added in my family and is really worth the few calories. Delicious with poultry or fish.

GELDERLAND OMELETTE
(PROVINCIAL OMELET)
1 lb. chopped mushrooms, sautéed in margarine
½ dozen eggs
1 cup milk

1 cup breadcrumbs
salt, pepper and paprika

Bring the milk to a boil and pour it hot over the breadcrumbs. Stir the eggs in a separate bowl and beat with a whisk for a few minutes. Now add the crumbs and milk, and season with salt, pepper and paprika. Add mushrooms. Fry the omelet gently in butter, lifting edges with spatula so it will not burn. Cut into quarters and serve. Serves 4.

I learned this recipe from a charming farm wife in Azewyn, Gelderland when I was 16. I never forgot it.

ZOETZUUR ROODE KOOL
(SWEET-SOUR RED CABBAGE)

1 firm red cabbage, washed and shredded
2 tbsps. vinegar
1 tbsp. sugar
4 tbsps. margarine
3 apples, diced
salt and pepper

Heat margarine. Add cabbage and cook 10 minutes with vinegar, then add other ingredients. Cover tightly, cook over low heat about 1 hour. Excellent as a side dish with all meats.

WITLOF (also called BRUSSELS LOF)
(ENDIVE CASSEROLE)

Buy several pounds of Belgian endive (when it is cheap!) and wash carefully. Put in pan with boiling water to cover, having added a pinch of salt. Cook until just tender, depending on thickness of stalks. Drain without separating stalks, and arrange in buttered baking pan. Sprinkle generously with breadcrumbs and dot *very generously* with butter or margarine. Brown in 375-degree oven for 20 minutes and serve with main meat dish.

This is the way endive is eaten throughout the Netherlands, and it is delicious.

AARDAPPEL-KAAS CROQUETTEN
(POTATO CROQUETTES WITH CHEESE)
(This recipe uses 2 of Holland's staple standbys: cheese and potatoes.)

      10-12 large potatoes, mashed and preferably hot
      1 cup shredded cheese (Gouda, Swiss or Cheddar)
      4 eggs, slightly beaten
      ½ tsp. white pepper
      2 tsp. salt
      1 cup milk in separate bowl
      1 cup breadcrumbs in another bowl
      vegetable oil in deep skillet

In large bowl, mix together the potatoes, eggs, cheese and spices. Shape into oval balls, roll in milk and then in crumbs. Brown for several minutes on all sides and drain on brown paper.

For a delicious variation, put a sliver of cheese inside each croquette before dipping in milk. It will melt partially and is delicious to bite into. Serve them piping hot with meats or salads. Serves 8.

KNOLLEN POT
(LEFTOVER TURNIP CASSEROLE)
This is great for the day after a turkey dinner!

Mix equal amounts of mashed potatoes and mashed yellow turnips with a cup of hot milk. Heat in oven in casserole, uncovered, so that top will brown. Dot with butter, sprinkle with chopped chives and a dash of nutmeg, salt and pepper.

KNOLLEN MOES
(RUTABAGA SOUFFLÉ)

2 cups soft bread- crumbs	4 cups cooked rutabaga (mashed)
½ tsp. ground mace	½ tsp. ground ginger

2 tbsps. sugar	2 eggs
1 cup milk	2 tbsps. butter or
	margarine

In good-sized bowl combine breadcrumbs, rutabaga, sugar, mace, ginger. In small bowl beat together milk and egg with fork. Stir into retabaga mixture. Pour into greased 2-qt. casserole, dot with butter and additional breadcrumbs. Bake at 350 degrees for 45 minutes. Top should be lightly brown. Yield: 5 to 6 servings.

UITSMYTER
(BOUNCER'S SNACK)

(This simple dish received its name because it was served traditionally to tavern patrons in order to sober them up and get them on their way home.)

2 slices white bread (not toasted), buttered
    generously
sliced cold roast beef or veal on top
2 eggs, fried gently in butter, for the top layer

Simple but delicious. My father had it regularly on Sunday evenings as a late bite.

BOEREN OMELETTE
(PEASANT-STYLE OMELET)

This recipe, often called omelette paysanne, comes from the Holland-Belgium border area, hence the French nickname. It is often served as a farm breakfast but can grace the most elegant buffet party when accompanied by a huge salad and a long loaf of crusty buttered bread.

6 eggs
½ cup diced salt pork or good back bacon
2 large raw potatoes, diced
2 tbsps. minced parsley
2 tbsps. butter

dash salt (optional because of salt pork)
chopped chives for garnish if desired

In omelet pan or good-sized skillet, melt 1 tbsp. of the butter and add the diced meat. When brown, remove to a plate and set aside. Add potatoes to fat and stir until golden. Have eggs lightly beaten in a bowl and add to them the meat, parsley and salt. Tilt pan and pour mixture in. When eggs start to set, pour in the remaining butter around edges and under omelet. Be careful to keep from sticking. When first delicious smell of eggs becomes apparent, turn omelet with spatula and let brown lightly on other side. When both sides are even, slide omelet carefully onto platter, garnish with chives and cut into 4 pieces. Pumpernickel bread is very tasty with this, and makes a complete hearty one-dish meal. Great also with leftover vegetables such as spinach or green beans.

HOOFDGERECHTEN
MAIN DISHES AND ENTRÉES

"Warm eten," or the hot meal, was served at midday for centuries. Pedal bicycles, the universal mode of transportation, brought the breadwinners and other family members home for a long dinner hour at that period of day, and even the schools closed down for that time.

Because cycling in all forms of weather saps an enormous amount of energy, the hot meal supplies the bulk of daily body fuel, and consists most often of a hearty soup, main course with side dishes, and a pudding-with-sauce dessert. What makes this meal important is that the morning breakfast or "koffietafel" consists simply of spice cake, cheese, bread and butter, and jams. The evening meal, called "boterham," or sandwich meal, was and is more of the same, with perhaps the additon of cold sliced meats and soft- boiled eggs.

The staple fare, therefore, whether enjoyed at midday or fashionably later, remains winter and summer a hearty repast, adequate to take the pedaling, walking or motoring Hollander back to complete the day's chores.

Oma's gehakt	Overschotpot
Boerenkool met rook- worst	Bloemkool met ham
Blinde vinken	Gevulde Tomaten
Hutspot	Vleesballen in roomsaus
Kip Croquetten	Luxe Kalfspot
Ham Schotel	Ragout croquetten
Gebraden gans	Haché
Appel-pruimen vulling	Echte Hollandse biefstuk #1
Appel-rozynen vulling	Echte Hollandse biefstuk #2
Heete Bliksem	
Gevulde Kalfsborst	Gefarceerde eieren
Biefstuk rollade	Zuurkool stamp
	Jachtschotel

OMA'S GEHAKT
(GRANDMOTHER'S MEATLOAF)

3 eggs	1 cup breadcrumbs
½ tsp. season salt	(flavored)
¼ tsp. thyme	½ tsp. freshly ground pepper
	1 can tomato sauce or Arturo sauce

37

| 1 small can chopped | 1 lb. pork sausage |
| mushrooms | 3 lbs. ground beef |

Mix all ingredients in order and shape into 1 large or 2 smaller loaves. Place in greased pan (uncovered) and roast for 1¼ hours at 375 degrees. During last 20 minutes of cooking put tomato slices on top. Delicious hot or cold.

BOERENKOOL MET ROOKWORST
(KALE-SAUSAGE CASSEROLE)

3 lbs. kale (fresh or frozen)
2 lbs. rookwurst (this may be smoked beef or
pork sausage, or Polish
Sausage, or knock wurst)
3 lbs. potatoes, boiled
1 stick butter or margarine
salt and pepper

Wash kale thoroughly if using fresh. Drain. Cover with boiling salted water ½ hour. Wash sausage, cook about 20 minutes in water. Drain and cut in coarse serving portions. Drain kale and chop. (Frozen kale is already chopped.) Mix with coarsely mashed potatoes, butter, salt and pepper. Top with meat and serve hot in casserole.

BLINDE VINKEN
(VEAL BIRDS)

1 lb. veal (boneless,	½ lb. ground beef
cut in 3″ squares)	
2 tbsps. parsley, minced	3 tbsps. onion, minced
½ tsp. minced garlic	½ tsp. salt
1 egg, beaten	3 tbsps. butter
dash pepper and thyme	
leaves	

In a mixing bowl, combine the beef, seasonings, garlic and onion. Add parsley. Mix. Arrange veal pieces on a floured board and put small mound of beef mixture in center of each. Roll the birds carefully and tie each with fine string or coarse white thread. (Toothpicks may be used but thread is more traditional).

Heat butter in skillet until brown, and add rolls, turning until brown on all sides. Cover skillet and cook slowly for 30 minutes. A little water or 2 tbsps. dry sherry may be added for a delicious jus. Serve with poppy-seed noodles or small white potatoes.

HUTSPOT
(CARROT HOTCHPOTCH)
(This is the all-Dutch winter meal.)

2-3 lbs. flank steak
1 qt. water
2 lbs. large carrots (we call them "winter carrots" in Holland.)
1 lb. yellow onions
2 lbs. boiling potatoes
salt and pepper
vinegar in small table carafe

Put the meat in a large kettle with the cold water. Bring to boil and turn to simmer immediately for ¾ hour. Then add potatoes, peeled and quartered. Carrots and onions now go on top. Cook about 20 minutes. Remove meat and liquid. Mash the vegetables with a coarse potato masher. Mix all thoroughly, season with salt and pepper. Slice meat and arrange around large platter with the *hutspot*. The Dutch always pass a small carafe of wine vinegar for individual serving. Incidentally, as a child I loathed and dreaded Saturdays in winter, because we invariably had *hutspot* and I hated it. Now I make it for my American family as a delicacy!

KIP CROQUETTEN
(DUTCH CHICKEN CROQUETTES)

2 tbsps. margarine or
    butter
1 cup milk

2 tbsps. flour
1 tsp Worcestershire

39

2 tsps. salt	2 eggs
1/8 tsp. paprika	1/8 tsp. pepper
1 tbsp. chopped parsley	2 cups chopped chicken
(fresh preferred)	breadcrumbs

Melt butter in saucepan, add flour and cold milk slowly until smooth and creamy. Add seasonings and parsley. Boil 3 minutes. Add chicken, mix well and pour out on large platter to cool. When cool enough to handle, take large spoonfuls of the mix in floured hands, shape into oval balls and put in refrigerator to firm. Roll in crumbs, then in eggs beaten with 2 tbsps. cold milk, then in crumbs again. Fry in deep fat and drain on brown paper. Should make 14 *croquetten.*

Recipe from Cornelia Renga who was born in Tilburg.

HAM SCHOTEL
(ESCALLOPED HAM DISH)

4 cups cold minced ham
2 cups bread crumbs
8 hardboiled eggs
1 tsp. paprika
1 tsp. mustard
3 tbsps. melted butter or margarine
1 scant qt. milk

Mix all dry ingredients and margarine, add milk, turn into buttered casserole. Sprinkle top generously with bread crumbs to which some more margarine has been added. Bake at 350 degrees for 1 hour. This dish is excellent for the day after Easter as it uses up the leftover ham and hard-boiled eggs.

GEBRADEN GANS
(ROAST GOOSE)

allow 1 to 1¼ lbs. of goose for each serving
a 3 lb. piece of pork in pan with goose for additional flavor
flour for dredging
salt and pepper

Use tender goose. Wash with weak solution of baking soda, then rinse. Fill with prune and apple stuffing. Sew up as you

40

would a turkey. Pierce breast to allow fat to escape. Put in a roasting pan, breast side down, sprinkle with salt and pepper and dredge lightly with flour. Put in hot oven at 450 degrees. When flour browns, add 2 cups of boiling water. Baste frequently. Cook 1 hour. Turn goose over and cook 40 minutes. One-half cup of white wine is to be added to pan ½ hour before finishing. Giblet gravy, apple sauce, or cranberries may be served with the goose.

APPEL-PRUIMEN VULLING
(PRUNE AND APPLE DRESSING)
(For Goose or Duck)
½ cup blanched almonds
6 apples
½ lb. prunes

Wash, pare and quarter apples. Soak prunes and remove pits. Blanch almonds. Combine apples, prunes and almonds, and stuff into goose or duck.

APPEL-ROZYNEN VULLING
(APPLE-RAISIN DRESSING)
6-8 apples, sliced thickly
1 cup raisins, presoaked in ½ cup sherry

Fill breast cavity of fowl. Be prepared for seconds. (I usually cook extra stuffing on the side!)

HEETE BLIKSEM
(HOT LIGHTNING)
(Traditional)
5 potatoes, peeled and cubed
2 onions, diced
5 apples, peeled and cubed
4 cups stock or 2 cans consommé and 1 can water
2 tsps. pepper (see note)
2 tbsps. salt
6 pork chops, 1 inch thick

41

12 pork sausages

Combine the potatoes, onions, apples, and stock in a saucepan. Cook over medium heat for 45 minutes, or until the liquid is absorbed. Sprinkle 1 tsp. of the pepper and the salt on the pork chops. Heat a skillet. Add the chops and fry until tender and well browned on both sides, about 30 minutes. In a separate frying pan, fry the sausages until browned. Drain well. Add the remaining pepper to the potato and apple mixture and stir. Form into a mound in the center of a platter. Arrange the pork chops and sausages around it.

GEVULDE KALFS BORST
(STUFFED BREAST OF VEAL)

½ lb. beef, ground
1 egg, beaten
4 tsps. salt
2 tsps. pepper
2 tbsps. chopped parsley
6 gherkins
2 hard-cooked eggs
1 breast of veal (with pocket for stuffing)
4 tbsps. butter
3 onions, sliced

Mix the ground beef, egg, 1½ tsps. of the salt, ¾ tsp. of the pepper, and the parsley together. Divide the mixture in half and shape each half to fit the pocket in the veal. On one of the halves, arrange the gherkins and eggs. Cover with the remaining half. Place in the veal pocket and fasten the opening with skewers or toothpicks. Sprinkle the remaining salt and pepper on the veal. Melt the butter in a roasting pan. Place the veal in it, with the onions arranged around the meat. Roast in a 350-degree oven for 3 hours, or until the veal is brown and tender. Baste frequently. Slice carefully between the ribs and serve.

BIEFSTUK ROLLADE
(STEAK ROLLS)

Flank or round steak, cut into strips about 4½" long

½ chopped onion for each
slice of lean bacon for each
ground pepper and nutmeg

Allow 2 rollades per person for robust appetites, 1 each for moderate eaters. Pound each steak strip with edge of a plate. Place bacon and onion on top, season with the nutmeg and pepper. Salt will not be needed because of the bacon. Roll up each strip and tie with clean thin string. Roast in moderate oven (350 degrees) for about 2 hours. May be basted with ½ cup of water added to the bacon drippings, and of course an equal amount of red wine is optional. Make sure they are fork-tender before serving.

OVERSCHOT POT
(LEFTOVER HOTPOT)

2-3 cups leftover beef, lamb or pork
3 tbsps. flour
4 or 5 link sausages (optional)
4 medium potatoes, sliced ¼ inch thick
2 apples, peeled and sliced
1 large onion, peeled and sliced
salt and pepper
about 2 cups tomato juice
3 beef bouillon cubes
pinch of sage or nutmeg

Cut meat in cubes and dredge with the flour. Cut sausages in half. In a casserole, put half of the mixed potato, apple and onion. Add meats, then rest of potato mix. Heat tomato juice, dissolve bouillon cubes in it. Add sage, salt and pepper. Pour over ingredients in casserole. Cover and bake at 350 degrees for about 1½ hours.

BLOEMKOOL MET HAM
(CAULIFLOWER-HAM CASSEROLE)

1 good-sized head cauliflower
2 cups leftover ham, cubed
½ lb. sliced fresh mushrooms (or 1 can, drained)
4 tbsps. butter or margarine

1/3 cup flour
1 cup milk
1 cup cubed cheese (cheddar is really tastiest)
½ cup dairy sour cream
1½ slices crumbled soft bread
1 tbsp. melted butter or margarine

Cut cauliflower in florets and cook, covered, in boiling salted water until tender. Do not overcook; drain. If using fresh mushrooms, steam or sauté for a few minutes. Combine mushrooms and ham. In a saucepan, melt the butter and stir in flour. Add the milk, cook and stir until mixture thickens and bubbles. Add cheese and let it melt; stir in sour cream. Combine carefully with cauliflower and the mushroom-ham mixture. Grease lightly a 2-qt. casserole and spoon the mixture in, taking care not to mash the cauliflower florets. In a small bowl, make a mix of the crumbs and remaining melted butter, and top casserole with this. Bake at 325 degrees for about 45 minutes. Will serve 6.

This dish was always served with Easter farm ham leftovers when I was in boarding school in the province of Gelderland. It is foolproof and delicious.

GEVULDE TOMATEN
(COLD STUFFED TOMATOES)

Peel tomato, remove thin slice from top. Remove seeds and some of the pulp. Sprinkle inside with salt. Turn upside down to drain for a few minutes. Fill with the following chicken salad mixture.

2 cups cooked fowl, diced
1 cup diced celery
¾ cup mayonnaise

Toss, then fill the tomato cavity. Place on crisp greens. Finish with a dash of paprika and a few sprigs of watercress or parsley (do not allow stuffing to come down on the tomato.)

VLEESBALLEN IN ROOMSAUS
(SPICED MEATBALLS IN CREAM)

2 lbs. lean ground beef
1 lb. ground pork
2 well-beaten eggs
1 cup mashed potatoes
1 cup breadcrumbs
1 tsp. brown sugar
½ tsp. each of ground cloves, allspice, ginger,
        pepper
1 cup milk
2 cups light cream (2 additional cups milk may
        be substituted for cream)

In large bowl work all ingredients together, except for cream. Mixture will be soft. Shape into small balls. Dust with flour, sauté in butter until brown. Transfer to baking casserole and pour in cream. Bake at 325 degrees for 35-40 minutes.

This recipe is great for using up leftover mashed potatoes. If you happen to have none on hand, another cup of breadcrumbs may be substituted.

LUXE KALFSPOT
(ELEGANT VEAL CASSEROLE)

2 lbs. veal steak (round is best), cut in strips
1½ tbsps. vegetable oil
1½ tbsps. butter or margarine
3 tbsps. flour
½ tsp. salt
¼ tsp. pepper
1½ cups water
1 chicken bouillon cube
6 small yellow onions, cut in eighths
½ cup (generous) Chablis or other white wine
2 tbsps. snipped parsley
2 bay leaves

In a large skillet, heat oil and margarine together. Add veal gradually and brown. Now, with wooden spoon, push meat to one side and blend in flour, salt and pepper with the drippings. Stirring, add water and bouillon cube until it boils. Lower heat and add onions, wine, bay leaves and parsley. Cover and continue low heat until tender, about ½ hour. Stir occasionally and do not allow to burn.

While veal is cooking, make a pot of hot-cooked white rice. Remove bay leaves from skillet, pour veal over rice. This will serve 4 generously, or 6 if you are on a budget or a diet. Pass a carafe of chilled Chablis.

RAGÔUT CROQUETTEN
(BEEF CROQUETTES)

Dice cooked soupmeat and follow same recipe as for *kip croquetten*. Serve with hot mustard or horse radish and pass plenty of crusty rye or pumpernickel.

HACHé
(LEFTOVER BEEF CASSEROLE)

This recipe is particularly popular in the southern provinces of Brabant and Limburg, hence the Flemish name borrowed from Belgium.

    4 cups (approx.) cold meat, cubed
    4 medium onions, sliced but not too thin
    1 tbsp. flour
    margarine for browning
    ½ cup wine vinegar
    ½ cup water
    1 tbsp. sugar

Brown onions in margarine (not too brown). Add meat which has been dredged in the flour. Brown together for a few minutes, add some salt and pepper. Add vinegar-water mix and cook over moderate flame for 1 hour or until tender. Add sugar and serve with poppy-seed noodles. This recipe is even tastier when done in the pressure cooker.

(Note: More vinegar and water may be added if too much has been absorbed in cooking.)

ECHTE HOLLANDSE BIEFSTUK
(REAL DUTCH STEAK)(Version # 1)
2 lbs. round steak, cut at least 1½ inches thick
½ tsp. salt
freshly ground pepper to taste
2 tbsps. vinegar
1 cup butter
about 1 cup water
½ cup parsley sprigs

Wipe steak with clean cloth and pound on both sides with an empty bottle or wooden mallet. Score deep diagonal slashes on both sides. In a cup, mix the vinegar and seasonings and rub both sides of meat. Let stand to marinate for half an hour. In a heavy skillet (iron is best) heat butter until hot but not burning. Sear steak on one side for a minute, turn and do the other side. This may be repeated until desired degree of rareness is reached. Lift steak onto a hot platter and set to back of stove. Now quickly stir the water into the pan, butter, and pour into a pre-warmed gravy boat. Sprinkle parsley over the steak and be sure the carver slices it diagonally and across the grain. Will serve six in Holland, and four in the U.S., where we are traditionally large meat devourers.

And now for a completely different version, depending on locale or what one mother or grandmother taught. The only things similar in both schools of thought are:

(1) Use *real* butter
(2) serve very rare and *hot*!
(3) accompany steak with potatoes and tiny peas

ECHTE HOLLANDSE BIEFSTUK
(REAL DUTCH STEAK) (VERSION # 2)

2 lbs. lean round steak   salt and pepper to taste
¼ cup milk   1 cup butter

Scrape the meat free of all surface matter and rub briskly with salt and pepper. Heat butter in iron skillet until hot. Using tongs, lower the meat into the butter, taking care *not* to pierce it. Sear the meat one minute on each side, and turn

47

until desired doneness. Remove meat with tongs and keep hot. Gently pour milk into the pan butter, heat but do not boil. Stir the gravy and pour it directly over the meat. Slice across the grain and serve with either boiled potatoes or sliced boiled and fried. (In the U.S. we call them home fries).

GEFARCEERDE EIEREN
(EGGS-IN-A-MUFF)

6 hard-boiled eegs, peeled
1 cup bread or crackercrumbs
1 egg-white, slightly beaten
butter or margarine for browning
meatloaf mixture, consisting of your own favorite ingredients, or the following:
1 lb. lean ground beef
½ lb. pork sausage
2 eggs
½ cup seasoned breadcrumbs
enough water to make a smooth mix

Make patty of the meat mixture large enough to roll the egg in. Place each egg on the patty and roll so that egg is hidden. Dip each roll in egg white and then in the cracker crumbs. Brown on all sides in skillet, add ½ cup of water (or beef stock if you have it) and cover over until done.

(Note: In Holland, there is a special mix called Paneermeel. In the U.S. we will use either cracker crumbs, breadcrumbs or rolled cornflakes.)

When done, they are served hot on cold lettuce leaves.

Mieke's Note: This traditional family recipe was given to me by my good friend Rita Waterman of South Weymouth, Massachusetts.

ZUURKOOLSTAMP
(TRADITIONAL SAUERKRAUT CASSEROLE)

This was another of my childhood recollections of Saturday fare. It is not a juvenile favorite and kept my New

York City schoolmates from hinting to be invited to "eat over" as they called it.

    6 to 8 large potatoes, peeled and quartered
    1 lb. sauerkraut
    2 lbs. smoked sausage

Put potatoes in huge kettle with water to cover. When they are semi-cooked, drain off half the water and add the sausage, cooking until potatoes are nearly done. Add sauerkraut on top and finish cooking. Pick out sausage with a huge fork and arrange on a platter. Mash thoroughly the potatoes and sauerkraut, add plenty of ground pepper. Salt should not be needed. Heap in center of sausages and serve with some ice-cold beer and some pumpernickel bread. Men love this dinner!

JACHTSCHOTEL
(HUNTER'S CASSEROLE)

    10 to 12 slices cooked cold beef, veal or pork
    2-3 large onions, thinly sliced
    8 large potatoes, boiled
    6 cooking apples, peeled and sliced
    1½ cups bouillon (or water with beef cube dissolved)
    freshly ground pepper
    minced parsley for garnish

In a skillet, lightly brown together the onions and apples. Butter a deep casserole and alternate slices of potato, meat and onion mixture in that order, making certain that the top layer will be potato. Pour the bouillon over and dot with butter and parsley garnish. Bake in a moderate oven for about 1 hour or until thoroughly piping hot and golden brown on top.

    (Note: This recipe may be varied without use of apples and by mashing instead of slicing the potatoes. It is then called *filosoof*, Philosophers' Casserole, and is also a great way to polish off leftovers.)

49

"STOVKIS BEUKEN, MIDDEN IN DE KEUKEN."
(Old fish-salting folksong)
FISH DISHES
(VIS SCHOTELS)

No Holland cookbook would be complete, or even accurate, without a sprinkling of fish recipes. Since the country was virtually scooped out of the sea, the eating and export of a wide variety of fish is a traditionally cultural staple of Netherlands heritage, and supplies much of the folklore and fable.

Herring is of course the prize catch, and by centuries-old tradition, the first and finest are barreled and sent within hours to the royal family. Then in early May, the streets and byways of Amsterdam, Scheveningen, Rotterdam and smaller towns are dotted with herring carts surrounded by eager customers.

The new young herring is so tender and succulent that it merely requires dipping in some finely chopped onion and guiding down the throat with very little chewing necessary. To eat it this way on the spot with head thrown back is the only way!

Alas, when most Holland fish reach export shores, they have been barreled and salted for preservation, and they do lose in the translation.

There are some other fish delicacies listed in the appetizer section of this book, but here I will include some of my favorite main dishes.

Visschotel met kaas	Koude vissla
Boeren kabeljauw	Gestoofde paling
Stovkis in wynsaus	Tong met dikke eiersaus

VISSCHOTEL MET KAAS
(FISH CASSEROLE WITH CHEESE)

6 good-sized fillets (flounder, sole or young cod)
1 cup dairy sour cream
½ cup cheese, slivered (Swiss or Gouda)
½ tsp. salt
freshly ground pepper
½ cup minced onion
1 tsp. mild mustard

Lightly grease a shallow baking pan. Preheat oven to 425 degrees. Arrange fillets without overlapping in bottom of pan. Combine cheese, onions and seasonings in a small bowl and spoon this mixture over the fish.

Baking time: about 20-25 minutes depending on the thickness of fillets. Test with fork for easy flaking. Do not overcook. May be put under broiler for 2 minutes to make top brown and bubbly.

BOEREN KABELJAUW
(COUNTRY-STYLE CODFISH)

2-lb. slice of cod-
fish in one piece
1 onion, sliced
½ tsp. thyme
2 bay leaves
1 cup dry white wine

1 carrot, sliced
2 tbsps. parsley
salt and pepper
4 tbsps. vegetable oil
3 tbsps. butter

With sharp knife, make a few gashes in sides of fish. Rub in salt and pepper. In deep bowl, put the oil, wine, carrot, onion, parsley, thyme, and bay leaves. Place fish in this mixture and allow to marinate for about 2 hours, turning as often as you think of it.

Put fish in a large shallow baking dish. Using strainer, pour marinating liquid over it and spread 1 tbsp. of the butter on top. Bake at 435 degrees for about 15 minutes, basting often with the marinade. Now remove from oven briefly and add remaining butter plus 2 tbsps. bread or cracker crumbs.

Return to oven for another 15 minutes. Small boiled potatoes may be arranged around it in the baking dish at this time. Sprinkle them with lemon, butter and parsley.

STOKVIS IN WYNSAUS
(HADDOCK OR HALIBUT CASSEROLE IN WINE)

4 good-sized halibut steaks
½ cup dry white wine (Sauterne or Chablis)
1 medium onion, sliced
½ cup celery, sliced
½ stick butter or margarine
2 tbsps. minced parsley
1 tsp. Worcestershire sauce
¼ tsp. basil leaves, crushed
2 medium tomatoes cut in sections

Salt and pepper the halibut steaks lightly. Place in shallow casserole, add wine. Allow to marinate for 30 minutes, turning once. In small skillet, cook celery and onion in the shortening until tender, stir in the basil, Worcestershire, and parsley. Pour this over fish and bake 10 minutes covered at 350 degrees. Uncover casserole, add tomatoes. Cover again and continue to bake another ten minutes or until fish flakes easily with fork. Serves 4.

TONG MET DIKKE EIERSAUS
(SOLE WITH CREAMY EGGSAUCE)

4 sole fillets	½ tsp. salt
¼ tsp. pepper	1 small onion, chopped
½ cup dry white wine	½ cup water
2 tbsps. butter or	2 tbsps. flour
margarine	¼ cup medium cream
1 egg yolk, beaten	
with fork	

In medium skillet or saucepan, place fillets, salt and pepper, water and wine, and bring to gentle boil. Cook about 10 minutes. In another pan, melt butter and add the flour. Drain the fish-cooking liquid into this and make a roux. Mix until smooth. Carefully add egg yolk and remove from heat immediately. Meantime, have heated serving platter ready for fish and arrange fillets on it. Add remaining butter and cream to the roux mixture and pour over the fish. This will serve 4.

KOUDE VISSLA ·
(COLD FISH SALAD)

(Believe it or not, this is delicious when made of leftover steamed or baked fish.)

1-2 cups (or more) leftover fish, diced or cut up
½ cup celery, diced
2 medium onions, minced (or 4 shallots, if possible)
2 tbsps. lemon juice
½ tsp. lemon juice
½ cup mayonnaise
freshly ground pepper

53

3 tbsps. capers for garnish (optional)

Mix all ingredients gently together, except capers because they crush. Let chill to blend seasonings. Spoon onto cold Boston or Bibb lettuce leaves and garnish with either the capers or tomato slices or both. And you thought you'd have to throw that leftover fish to the cat?

GESTOOFDE PALING
STEWED EEL

2 lbs. fresh Eel   1 lemon, sliced
3 tbsps. butter or margarine   pepper, salt
                                                   breadcrumbs

Clean the eel and cut into 3 to 4-inch pieces. Wash the pieces and rub in with salt and pepper. Place eel in baking dish and dot with the butter. Sprinkle breadcrumbs over all and place lemon slices on top. Place covered dish in moderate over (350 degrees F) for 15 minutes. Baste occasionally with the juice.

Mieke's note: This recipe comes to me from the kitchen of my Holland-born pen pal Tonia Teernstra of Ann Arbor, Michigan. I have her permission to use it in this book.

SAUSEN
(SAUCES)

The sauce or gravy that enhances the entrée is the secret pride of the Dutch homemaker and chef, and the ingredients that make up the formula are as well-guarded as are those of the French neighbors to the South. That which turns the ordinary into the *delicatesse* is often a simple addition of spice or staple. (Nutmeg of course is the national spice and is used in and on practically everything!) Some sauces, however, have become traditional and are served as reliables in all the provinces:

Zuure eierensaus	Tartaresaus
Mosterdsaus	Uienjus
Witte saus	Hollandse mayonnaise
Botersaus	Luxe puddingsaus

MOSTERDSAUS
(HOT MUSTARD SAUCE)
(From Apeldoorn)

2 tbsps. dry mustard	½ cup sugar
¼ cup vinegar	2 egg yolks
½ pt. cream	

Mix dry ingredients, mix eggs with cream. Put all in double boiler and add vinegar slowly. Excellent with ham or cold leftover beef.

ZUURE EIEREN SAUS
(HOLLANDAISE)
(Southern Provinces)

4 egg yolks	½ tsp. salt
1/8 tsp. cayenne pepper (or less)	1 cup hot melted butter
	2 tbsps. lemon juice

Beat egg yolks in an electric blender until quite thick and lemon colored. Add salt and cayenne.

Add 1/3 of butter slowly to above, beating constantly. When well blended, beat in rest of the butter alternately with the lemon juice a little at a time. Sauce may be made ahead of time and kept in refrigerator. When ready to serve, place container in lukewarm water and stir until softened.

WITTE SAUS
(BASIC WHITE SAUCE)
(This is used widely in the Netherlands for many vegetables.)

3 tbsps. butter or margarine

2 cups milk

3 tbsps. flour

salt and pepper to taste

In saucepan, melt butter, add half the flour, then half the milk, stirring constantly. Add the rest gradually, keep stirring, simmer 2-3 minutes. Add seasonings and remove from heat. May be made thin or thick depending on quantity of milk used.

BOTERSAUS
(SPICED BUTTER GRAVY)
½ cup butter (I have used margarine just as well.)

1 tsp. paprika

2 tsps. finely chopped parsley

1/8 tsp. ground mace

½ tsp. each of onion salt, garlic salt, celery salt

Melt butter in small saucepan. Do not let it brown! Add other ingredients. Serve hot over potatoes, egg noodles, or any type of cooked fish.

HOLLANDSE TARTARE SAUS
(DUTCH SAUCE TARTARE)
1 cup mayonnaise

½ cup capers (optional)

½ cup chopped chives or scallions

small bunch parsley, minced

4 or 5 sweet pickles, finely chopped

Mix all together gently so as not to break capers. Add freshly ground pepper. Serve with all seafoods, especially scallops or shrimp.

Note: Onions may be substituted for scallions.

ZUURE UIEN JUS
(TART ONION GRAVY)

Slice one medium-sized onion and brown in a generous pat of butter or margarine. Add a tbsp. of flour, a pinch of salt and stir. Add 1 cup bouillon, stock or hot water into which you have dissolved 2 beef bouillon cubes. Boil up quickly, remove from heat and add 1 tbsp. vinegar. This is a sure-fire success with boiled beef or pot roast, and especially *heete bliksem*. (See recipe.)

HOLLANDSE MAYONNAISE
(DUTCH MAYONNAISE)

4 egg yolks	½ tsp. salt
¼ tsp. dry mustard	¼ tsp. white pepper
1½ cups oil	4 tbsps. white vinegar

In good-sized bowl beat egg yolks and seasonings with a whisk or hand-mixer. Add oil carefully drop by drop until 2 tbsps. are in. Add 4 tbsps. vinegar. Continue to beat, adding remaining oil in steady stream. Mayonnaise may be thinned with milk to achieve sauce consistency if desired for pouring over fish, eggs, etc. Will keep indefinitely in refrigerator.

LUXE PUDDINGSAUS
(DELUXE DESSERT SAUCE)

3 eggs	2 tbsps. sugar
½ cup heavy cream	3 tbsps. sherry

In top part of double boiler (over boiling water), beat together the eggs, cream, and sugar. Stir constantly with wooden spoon, and when it thickens beat in the sherry. This sauce is very rich and is best served over a bland pudding such as vanilla or *blanc mange*. It is a Dutch favorite.

PUDDINGS EN NAGERECHTEN
(PUDDINGS AND DESSERTS)

In Holland, no true main meal is complete without the punctuating "amen" of the perfect pudding. Whether it be light after an elaborate meal, or rich after a small supper, the Dutch kitchen attaches much importance to it. In this section are some of the more traditional favorites:

Wentelteefjes   Mocha souffle
Haagse bluf   Banaan fritur
Hangop   Gember souffle
Rozynen-broodpudding   Choco-hazelnoot pudding
Chipolata

WENTELTEEFJES
(BREAD CREPES)
(Traditional)
This is an excellent late-evening snack for holidays. We always had it on St. Nicholas and Christmas eves.

58

Holland's
cheeses

gouda

LIMBURGSE
KAAS
VOLVET

GOUDA

KUMMEL

RADEMAKER'S
HAAGSCHE
HOPJES

HOLLAND

FOODS ¥
The PROVINCES
Deventer koek
Huzarensla
Zult
Boter wafels
Haagse Hopjes
Groninger koek
Nieuwe Haring
Botersprits
Rysttafel
and
CHEESE-CHEESE-CHEESE

Concerts SYMPHONY SOLOIST

MODEL for ILLUSTRATIONS COVERS

OVERSEAS TOUR for the ARMED FORCES

CHRISTMAS SHOW ~ RADIO CITY MUSIC HALL

Off Broadway: THE MERRY WIDOW

U.N. CONCERT (with DELEGATE)

HOLLAND AT THE FAIR

For Kodak: European Festival At Grand Central

MIEKE: Some career HIGHLIGHTS...

New York Opera Theater (6 leading ROLES) above as Mimi in 'LA BOHÈME'

Singer/Author Mieke in a few

BERMUDA MUSIC FESTIVAL (3 seasons)

CAVALCADE of STARS Town Hall, New York

MIRTH in MUSIC/Comedy TV

Mieke on "GOOD MORNING" with JANET LANGHART

COMMERCIALS for TEA, COSMETICS, CHEESE

with NINA (HARP) 8 seasons folk tours

and-on monitor records

MIEKE SAYS Cheese

AS A COMIC OPERA CHARACTER in "MUSICAPERS"

of her career highlights.

TRANSPORTATION

TROLLEY/TRAMS
SHIPS & SAILS
KLOMPEN (plain or carved)
BOATS & BARGES
SKATES & ICE-KITES
RAILROADS
CARS & BUSES
AIRPLANES
DOG & BIKE CARTS
BICYCLES !!!!!!

12 slices white bread (crusts cut away)
6 eggs
4 cups milk
1 tsp. vanilla
mixed sugar and cinnamon

Place bread slices on shallow platter. Beat eggs and add milk, then vanilla. Pour over bread and let soak 20 minutes. Fry gently in butter or margarine, turning once with spatual when golden. Sprinkle with cinnamon-sugar mixture and serve hot. Serves 12 (or should!).

HAAGSE BLUF
(SHOW-OFF DESSERT)

People who live in The Hague are traditionally teased by their neighbors as being show-offs or stuck-ups. The following fluffy dessert gives humorous truth to the legend—it is frothy, delicious, and practically nothing!

4 egg whites
2 cups finely granulated sugar
3/4 cup fruit syrup (any flavor—the Dutch use
red currant, "roode bessensap")

Pour the syrup, sugar, and egg whites in a bowl and beat with a hand-mixer at whipping speed. Lower speed and beat another minute, the tradition being that, the longer the whipping, the sweeter and more plentiful the dessert. Serve chilled in parfait or sherbet glasses with thin sweet wafers.

HANGOP
(BUTTERMILK PUDDING)

Many a Friday afternoon my brothers and I would come home from school and head for the old marble kitchen sink in New York, only to find the linen towel tied there, dripping the *hangop*!!! Hated it then but love it now.

2 qts. buttermilk
½ cup sugar
1 tsp. cinnamon
Holland Rusk, whitebread toast, or large soda
crackers

Line a colander with a wet linen napkin or towel. Pour in the buttermilk and let it drain for several hours by tying a string around the ends and fastening so that they can drip freely. When it is the consistency of pudding, put in a bowl and whip with a whisk, adding the sugar and cinnamon. Serve in deep dessert bowls with the crumbled rusks on top, and be sure it is really chilled. More cinnamon may be added to taste. Serves 6 generously.

ROZYNEN-BROOD PUDDING
(BREAD-RAISIN PUDDING)

4 slices buttered toast, quartered
1/3 cup raisins
2 eggs, slightly beaten
5 tsps. sugar, divided
1/8 tsp. salt
1 cup milk
1 cup boiling water
1 tsp. vanilla extract
1/4 tsp. cinnamon

In a buttered 1½ qt. casserole, place toast and sprinkle with raisins. In a small bowl, combine eggs, 4 tsps. of the sugar, salt, milk, water, and vanilla. Pour over toast and let stand 10 minutes. Sprinkle with mix of cinnamon and remaining sugar. Bake at 350 degrees for 30-40 minutes, or until knife comes out clean.

Mieke's Note: Our good friend Frank Scott of West Redding, Connecticut, was born in The Hague. He remembers this as a childhood recipe.

MOCHA SOUFFLÉ
(COFFEE SOUFFLÉ)

3 tbsps. butter
¾ cup strong coffee
½ cup sugar
4 eggs

3 tbsps. bread flour
1/3 cup light cream
¼ tsp. salt
½ tsp. vanilla

Melt butter, add flour and gradually add hot coffee and cream. Cook the mixture until it is smooth and thick. Beat egg yolks, sugar and salt together. Add the first mixture gradually to these ingredients. Beat until blended. Place over a low fire or in double boiler. Stir and cook for about one minute to permit the yolks to thicken slightly. Cool. Whip whites of eggs until stiff. Fold into the cooled mixture. Bake in a seven-inch baking dish in a moderate oven 325 degrees for about 35 minutes. Serve at once with coffee or mocha sauce.

GEMBER SOUFFLÉ
(GINGER SOUFFLÉ)

3 tbsps. flour	3 tbsps. butter or margarine
½ cup crystallized	1 cup milk
ginger	1 tbsp. sherry
1/3 cup sugar	¼ tsp. ground ginger
dash of salt	
4 egg yolks—4 egg	
whites	

In saucepan melt butter, stir in flour. Add milk to make a roux. Continue stirring and add crystallized and ground ginger, sugar, sherry, and salt. Remove from heat and beat in egg yolks, one at a time. Beat hard after each. Let cool. In clean medium bowl, beat egg whites, fold into ginger mix. Pour mix into buttered 2-qt. soufflé dish. Bake at 375 degrees for 40 minutes. Delicious when served warm.

BANAAN FRITUUR
(BANANA FRITTERS)

½ cup flour	¼ tsp. salt
4 egg yolks	2 tbsps. melted butter
1 cup milk	or oil
5-6 medium bananas, sliced	2 egg whites

Sift flour and salt in large bowl. With large spoon make a well in center and add egg yolks and melted shortening. Gradually add milk and mix to form smooth batter. Beat thoroughly, using hand-mixer if desired. Let stand in cool place for ½ hour. In clean bowl, beat egg whites stiff and fold in. Fold in sliced bananas. In shallow skillet, have one inch of cooking oil and bring to medium heat. Drop mixture by large spoonfuls into shortening and turn once when golden brown. Drain on brown paper.

This makes an excellent children's party lunch when sprinkled with confectioner's sugar.

CHOCOLADE-HAZELNOOT PUDDING
(HAZELNUT CHOCOLATE PUDDING)

2 tbsps. cocoa	½ cup chopped hazelnuts
½ cup brown sugar	½ cup milk
1 cup flour	¼ tsp. salt
2 tbsps. margarine	1¼ cups sugar, divided
an additional 1/3 cup cocoa	1½ cups boiling water

In medium bowl cream 3/4 cups sugar and margarine until fluffy, stir in milk. In another bowl sift together the flour, baking powder, salt, and 2 tbsps. cocoa. Add dry mix to cream mix and blend. Fold in hazelnuts and pour in greased 9-inch square pan.

Mix together the 1/3 cup cocoa, the brown sugar, and remaining ½ cup sugar, blend well. Sprinkle this over the batter in pan. Pour the boiling water over entire mixture. Bake at 350 degrees 35-40 minutes.

CHIPOLATA
(CHIPOLATA PUDDING)

2 envelopes gelatin
1½ oz. lady fingers
¼ cup liqueur (Kirsch, rum, Triple Sec, or
    something similar to your taste. I
    used Triple Sec.)

3 tbsps. currants
3 tbsps. raisins
2 tbsps. finely chopped candied orange peel
3 or 4 tbsps. chopped almonds
1½ cup milk
3/4 cup cream
4 eggs
½ cup sugar

Soften the gelatin in a small amount of water. Soak the ladyfingers, broken into pieces, in enough of the liqueur to cover. Cook the raisins and currants gently in water until they swell.

Separate the eggs. Combine the egg yolks with the sugar.

Combine the milk and cream and bring to the boiling point. Add the yolks and sugar mixture (it's better to add the milk and cream to the yolks and sugar rather than vice-versa) and heat gently for a few minutes until smooth. Add gelatin and heat until thoroughly dissolved.

Drain currants and raisins and add to mixture. Add the nuts and orange rind and the remaining liqueur.

Let this sit and stir every now and then until the raisins, etc., stay in a suspension somewhat and don't sink to the bottom. (I did this at room temperature, but it might be more effective to do it in the refrigerator.)

Fill a mold with this mixture in two layers, with a layer of the ladyfingers in between.

Note: The egg whites in this recipe were not used. My husband says that a real *chipolata* pudding should be fluffy, which indicates that perhaps the whites should have been beaten and folded in. At any rate, the recipe as written is quite delicious. Whether it would be better with the egg whites I don't know.

Mieke's Note: The above recipe was given to me by my good friend Marilyn Bakker of West Redding, Connecticut. I have her permission to use it in this book.

BROOD, TAART, KOEKJES
(BREAD, CAKE, COOKIES)

Holiday and carnival treats are included among the traditional baked goodies in this chapter. Many of these recipes are remembered from childhood and refreshed by Holland cousins as to content and authenticity, give or take a few grams and liters as translated into cup measure and level teaspoons!

Kaas en perenvla

Zoentjes

Appel beignets

Ontbyt broodjes

Knollenbrood

Appel Taart

Thee hapjes

Roomsoezen en Moor-
koppen

Kerstkrans

Sneeuwballen

Oliebollen

Echte ontbytkoek

Yoghurt Taart

Poffertjes

Speculaas

Jan Hagel

Boterkoek

Chocolade slagroomtaart

Filled speculaas cookies

Borstplaat

KAAS EN PERENVLA (Limburg)
(PEAR CHEESE PIE)

4 cups sliced peeled firm pears
3/4 cup sugar
3 tbsps. all-purpose flour
¼ tsp. nutmeg
¼ tsp. cinnamon
dash of salt
grated rind and juice of 1 lemon
pastry for 2-crust 9-inch pie
1 tbsp. butter
½ cup grated sharp cheddar cheese

Mix pears, sugar, flour, spices and salt. Add lemon rind and juice. Put in pastry-lined 9-inch piepan. Dot with butter and sprinkle with cheese. Adjust pastry strips on pie, lattice fashion. Bake in hot oven (425 degrees F.) 20 minutes. Reduce heat to 350 degrees; bake about 20 minutes. Serve slightly warm or cold. Grated sharp cheddar cheese may be sprinkled on pie filling before adjusting lattice strips. Traditional tea treat in this province.

ZOENTJES
(KISSES)

4 egg whites
4 tbsps. powdered sugar

Beat egg whites and sugar together until stiff. Drop by teaspoonfuls on greased cookie sheets or shallow foil pans. Literally *dry them* in an *oven* for 3 hours at 250 degrees. They should not brown. Makes several dozen, and they are great for children's parties, tea, or dessert when served with fruit.

APPEL BEIGNETS
(COURTESY NETHERLANDS CHAMBER OF COMMERCE)

Wash, peel and core about 6 apples. Cut crosswise into thick slices. Cover with confectioners' sugar moistened with a few tablespoons brandy or rum. A few minutes before serving, drain slices, dip in batter and fry in deep hot fat until

65

golden. Drain, place on fireproof platter, sprinkle with sugar, and set under high broiler heat a few minutes to glaze.

Batter:

1 cup all-purpose
  flour, sifted
2 tbsp. sugar
1 cup milk

½ tsp. salt
1 slightly beaten egg
1 tbsp. melted shortening

ONTBYT BROODJES
(BREAKFAST MUFFINS)

3 cups sweet milk
2 eggs beaten stiff
1 tbsp. sifted sugar
¼ tsp. soda

1 tbsp. melted butter
3 tbsps. good yeast
1 tsp. salt
enough flour to make batter
  stiff

Make all the ingredients, except the eggs and soda, into a stiff sponge and set to rise over night. Half an hour before serving, add the eggs and soda, dissolved in water. Bake in muffin rings on a hot griddle.

KNOLLEN BROOD
(TURNIP LOAF)

1 2/3 cups flour
½ tsp. soda
½ tsp. ground cloves
dash nutmeg
1/3 cup brown sugar
¼ cup orange juice
1/3 cup chopped dat.
1½ cups rutabaga,
  peeled and diced

1 tsp. baking powder
¾ tsp. salt
½ tsp. cinnamon
1 cup sugar
2 eggs, beaten
¼ cup melted butter or
  margarine
1/3 cup chopped walnuts

Cook rutabaga in small amount boiling water until tender. Drain and mash—you should have 1 cup. In mixing bowl, sift flour, soda, baking powder, salt, and spices. Next add sugar. In another bowl, combine mashed rutabaga, orange juice, eggs, and butter. When mixed add nuts and dates. Stir this mixture quickly into dry ingredients. Pour quickly into greased loaf pan (9″ by 5″). Bake at 350 degrees for 60-70 minutes. Insert large fork to test for doneness.

APPEL TAART
(APPLE TART)

¼ lb. sifted flour
2 tbsps. sugar
2 cups sweetened
    apple sauce

¼ lb. butter
milk
apples sliced thin
melted apricot jam (optional)

Blend butter with flour and sugar, add milk and mix into a dough. Roll and line a greased tart dish about an inch high, with thin dough layer patted down. Next put a layer of applesauce in tart shell and place apple slices over sauce. Bake about 12 minutes in moderate oven, 375 degrees. Spread melted apricot jam over apples. Serve cold with cream or ice cream.

THEE HAPJES
(TEA SCONES)

2 cups flour
1 tsp. salt
2 tsps. baking powder
½ cup finely chopped
    nuts

1 cup milk
2 tbsps. sugar
3 eggs, separated
4 tbsps. melted butter or
    margarine

Sift together the flour, salt, and sugar. In another bowl, beat together the egg yolks and milk, then pour this into dry ingredients and mix well. Add the baking powder and nuts; mix. Beat egg whites separately and fold into the batter. Pour into greased muffin pans and let bake in preheated oven, about 350 degrees, for 20-25 minutes. May be eaten warm with jam, or buttered.

OLIEBOLLEN
(CARNIVAL DOUGHNUTS)

3 cups sifted flour
1 pkg. powdered dry
  yeast
¼ cup sugar
1 egg
Powdered sugar for
  sprinkling

1 cup milk
½ tsp. nutmeg
3/4 tsp. salt
¼ cup vegetable oil
  (not olive)

In large mixing bowl combine 1 3/4 cups of the flour, the yeast, and nutmeg. In medium saucepan put milk, sugar, oil, and salt, and heat just until warm. Fold this into yeast mixture, add the egg. Beat for ½ minute with electric mixer at low speed, scraping sides of bowl. Now beat 3 minutes at high speed. Add remaining flour by tablespoons until you have a soft dough. Turn mixture into greased bowl, cover and chill for 2 hours. On well-floured surface, turn dough out and form into ball. Cover with large bowl for 10 minutes. With floured rolling pin, roll dough to large rectangle, about 12" x 18". Cut to size of oblong dinner rolls. Cover again and let rise another half hour. Heat fat to 375 degrees in deep skillet and fry 4 or 5 *oliebollen* at a time for about 1 minute or until golden. May be turned once. Scoop out with slotted spoon and dry on brown paper. Dust with powdered sugar if desired. You should have about 3 dozen.

Oliebollen are served traditionally at every *kermis* (carnival) throughout the Netherlands and are sold directly from a cart.

ECHTE ONTBYTKOEK
(REAL BREAKFAST SPICECAKE)

(This is the traditional standby on every Koffietafel in Holland.)

2 cups sifted flour
1 cup milk
½ cup molasses
1 tsp. cinnamon
1½ tsps. ginger

1 tsp. baking powder
½ cup brown sugar
½ tsp. ground nutmeg
1 tsp. ground cloves

Butter a loaf pan and heat oven to 300 degrees. In a good-sized bowl, combine first the dry ingredients, then add the milk and molasses. Pour batter in pan and bake for 1 hour. Allow to cool on a rack, and keep it moist by wrapping in foil or keeping in a covered tin as all my cousins do. The kitchen will smell divine while this is baking, so be sure to make extra loaves for another day or another family! Keeps well and is delicious when buttered.

YOGHURT TAART
(YOGHURT TART)

1 qt. yoghurt
juice of one lemon
one egg
11 oz. can of tangerine sections
1 envelope gelatin
sponge cake (or graham-cracker crust)

For a few hours, let the yoghurt sit in a strainer lined with cheesecloth. (If cheesecloth is unavailable, a heavy-duty paper towel does fine.) During this time, quite a lot of moisture will drip out of the yoghurt. About 1½ cups of yoghurt will be left in the strainer.

There is about ½ cup juice in the can of tangerine sections. Dissolve the gelatin in the juice and heat until thoroughly dissolved.

Mix the yoghurt, well-beaten egg, lemon juice, and tangerine juice with gelatin. Fold in the tangerine slices.

In Holland, you can buy ready-made sponge-cake "bottoms" in the market.

Here, a spring-pan bottom can be lined with sponge cake. A commercial layer seems too thick. I slice a commercial layer horizontally and place it in the bottom of a spring-pan. If the cake is too small, the bottom can be filled in with pieces of sponge cake left over from the cut-off top. After the bottom of the spring pan is lined with sponge cake, pour the yoghurt mixture on top. Allow to harden in the refrigerator.

An alternative to the sponge-cake bottom is a ready-made graham-cracker crust, but this is not as *lekker* as the cake.

Mieke's Note: The above recipe was given to me by my good friend Marilyn Bakker of West Redding, Connecticut. I have her permission to use it in this book.

69

POFFERTJES

These are traditional Dutch *kermis* (carnival) treats and just simply cannot be translated or imitated. There are several variations, but this one comes from the *kermis* in Tilburg, my mother's hometown in the province of Noord Brabant. If you have been to Holland and have located a real *poffertjes* pan with the 7 wells, lucky you! The antique ones are expensive and hard to find, but the newer ones do well too, and are easier to clean.

2 generous cups
   flour, sifted
1 cup beer
pinch salt (optional)

5-6 egg yolks
1 cup whole milk
raisins (optional)

In a good-sized bowl, mix the flour, egg yolks and liquids, beating well after each addition. If you have no real *poffertjes* pan, do the next best thing by putting heaping tablespoons of the batter on a greased griddle, and use a little less milk so batter is a bit thicker. Turn when bubbly, and serve piping hot with powdered sugar and huge paper napkins. (Note: At the Middelburg *kermis* in Zeeland, they served us these with a delicious addition of rum-soaked raisins and citron.)

SPECULAAS
(TRADITIONAL ST. NICHOLAS HOLIDAY COOKIE)

4 cups all-purpose
   flour
1 cup soft butter
1 cup light brown sugar,
   firmly packed
4 tbsps. baking powder
1 tsp. salt
1 tbsp. cinnamon

½ cup almonds, blanched
1 tsp. ground cloves
1 tsp. ground nutmeg

½ tsp. pepper

½ tsp. ground anise seed
scant ½ cup milk

Combine all ingredients except almonds. Knead into a soft dough. Roll with floured pin on floured board or wax paper. Thickness should be ½ inch or so. If you have a press that makes traditional holiday designs, wonderful! With a cutter, make cookies about 3" x 2", or if you prefer round, make them about the same in diameter. Slide onto greased cookie sheets into a preheated 350-degree oven for about 25 minutes. Oh I nearly forgot, press a whole almond or two into each one before baking. They will be golden brown and you should have from 3 to 4 dozen depending on size. They keep beautifully in a covered tin, but they won't last!

JAN HAGEL
(TRADITIONAL SHORTBREAD COOKIE)

1 egg, separated
1 cup sugar
1 cup soft butter

1 tbsp. water
¾ tsp. cinnamon
½ cup chopped almonds

Cream together the butter, sugar and egg yolk. Sift together the flour and cinnamon and add to butter mix. Grease a 9" x 13" x 2" baking pan and spread the mixture in it evenly, patting it down with a large flat spoon. Now beat together the water and egg white and brush evenly over the dough. Add nuts and press in lightly if desired. Bake for half an hour in a preheated 350 degree oven until it is lightly browned. While still hot, cut into 2" x 3" bars and put pan to cool. Separate when cool and store in a tin. Makes from 2 to 3 dozen depending on the size you cut them. Delicious with tea or cocoa.

ROOMSOEZEN EN MOORKOPPEN
(CREAM PUFFS AND BLACKBONNETS)

½ cup sweet butter
1 tsp. sugar
1 cup flour (not self-
  rising)

1 cup hot water
¼ tsp. salt
4 eggs

In a saucepan, pour the hot water over the butter and stir until butter melts. Add salt and sugar and bring to a rapid boil. Dump in the flour and raise saucepan from heat, stirring with rapid strokes (wooden spoon) until mixture leaves sides of pan, forming a ball in the center. Remove pan from heat and add the eggs unbeaten and one at a time, beating vigorously after each. Heat oven to 400 degrees. Grease 2 large baking sheets and drop batter onto them by round tablespoonfuls. Bake for 10 minutes and then lower oven to 350. Bake from 30 to 40 minutes or until puffs show no beads of moisture. Remove from oven and allow to cool. Split with sharp knife and fill with sweetened whipped cream. Note: When coated with a chocolate glaze, they are called Moorkoppen, or blackamoor heads.

CHOCOLADE SLAGROOMTAART
(WHIPPED CREAM CHOCOLATE CAKE)

1 cup sugar	½ cup boiling water
¼ cup butter	1 egg, well beaten
¼ cup buttermilk	1 cup all-purpose flour
2 squares melted bitter chocolate	¾ tsp. baking soda
	1 tsp. baking powder

In a large mixing bowl, dump without stirring the sugar, butter, buttermilk and melted chocolate. Next add the boiling water and *stir*. Next mix in the well-beaten egg, and add the flour which has been sifted with the soda and baking powder. Beat until smooth and light with hand mixer. Line the bottom of a 9-inch square pan (or equivalent size) with a sheet of oiled wax paper. Bake in 375-degree oven for 30-45 minutes. Test by pressing lightly on top, or insert toothpick to come out clean. Turn cake onto a rack to cool. Whip ½ to 1 cup heavy cream with ½ tsp. vanilla and 1 tbsp. sugar. Apply cream topping only when cool and serve immediately.

Note: Recipe may easily be doubled to make a layer cake. Cream topping will then be between layers and generously on top. This cake is easy for beginners and foolproof.

GEVULDE SPECULAAS
(FILLED SPECULAAS COOKIES)

Have on hand 2 cookie sheets 13" x 9" x 2"

Filling:

1 lb. almond paste	3 eggs (beaten)
2 cups sugar	½ tsp. lemon extract

Mix all these ingredients well; let stand overnight

Speculaas dough:

1 lb. butter	2 tsp. cinnamon
4 cups flour	½ tsp. cloves
1 tsp. baking soda	½ tsp. nutmeg
2 cups sugar	2 tsp. milk

Divide speculaas dough in 4 parts; 2 for each cookie sheet. One part goes on bottom of pan. Pat out with hand. Add layer of filling, then put second part of dough on top. (This is best done between 2 pieces of waxed paper using a rolling pin. Do same with second cookie pan.

Brush with a beaten egg to which a little sugar has been added. Sprinkle with slivered almonds and bake in 350 degree oven for 35-40 minutes.

The same dough may also be used for regular speculaas cookies without the filling. These will be thin and crispy.

Mieke's note: This recipe was given to me for this book by Mrs. Roland Krygsman of Clifton, New Jersey. She was born in a small village on an island in Zeeland province. The town is Ooltgensplaat and the island is Goeree-en-Overflakkee.

An interesting custom in this village was the traditional "poterbal" festival. Small seed potoes would be cooked in hot bacon grease and it was a great neighborhood event in which all participated.

P.S.: There are over 80 potato varieties in Holland!

BUTTER CAKE
(BOTERKOEK)

½ cup cold butter   ½ cup cold margarine
1 egg   ¼ tsp. baking powder
2 cups all-purpose flour   ¾ cup granulated sugar
1 egg yolk   almonds (peeled)

Mix first six ingredients well and press with fingertips into baking dish. Flatten smooth with spatula. Press in almonds. Mix egg yolk with a few drops of water and brush this over mixture. Bake for about 45 minutes in moderate oven (325 degrees F.)

SNEEUWBALLEN

(New Year's Eve Snowballs)

Make basic cream puff dough (p. 71). Drop by tablespoons into deep hot fat. They should be round, not oblong. Fry until puffed and golden on all sides. Drain on paper towels and cool.

With the point of a pastry bag, push a small hole in the side of each snowball, and fill with sweetened whipped cream. Sprinkle thickly with confectioners' sugar. Stack in a mound and serve.

TEATIME in Holland is a dedicated and serious business. Relatives and close friends even keep a personal teacup at each-other's homes. But..no one drinks what is humorously called "een naakte tas thee" (a naked cup of tea). One or more of these cakes or confections will always be ready to serve on accompanying little trays.

LETTERBANKET or KERSTKRANS

(Sinterklaas Initials; Christmas Wreath)

This renowned Dutch pastry, made of puff paste with an almond paste filling, is traditional both on Sinterklaas Eve and at Christmas. At Sinterklaas it is shaped in the family initial (s), at Christmas it is given the form of a wreath and decorated with glaceed fruit.

Puff Pastry:
> ½ cup (1 stick) sweet butter
> 1 cup sifted all-purpose flour
> ¼ cup (or more) ice water
> pinch of salt

Almond Paste Filling:
> ¼ lb. blanced almonds
> ½ cup sugar
> 1 egg
> pinch of salt
> grated peel of 1 lemon

Make puff paste dough following basic cookbook directions. While it chills, prepare the almond paste. Grind the blanched almonds and mix with the sugar, beaten egg, grated peel and salt. Grind this mixture once more. On a floured board, foll it into a number of 'sausages' about 1" in diameter. Wrap in waxed paper and chill.

After the final chilling period, roll out the dough into a strip 3½" wide and 1/8" thick. Place sausages end to end along the center, fold dough over it and seal top and ends with water. Shape into the required initial and place it, seam down, on a floured cookie sheet. Brush with beaten egg diluted with water. Bake 30 - 35 minutes in 425° oven. Cool on rack.

For the Christmas wreath, shape the filled strip into a ring, sealing ends together. Bake as above; cool. Spread with confectioners' icing and decorate lavishly with red and green glacéed cherries and leaves cut from candied citron.

BORSTPLAAT

(Sinterklaas Fondants)

Literally translated, borstplaat means chest plate; no one seems to know why. It is one of a rich variety of traditional Sinterklaas candies. For the large thick ones, special ring molds are available in Holland, but flat lids of cookie tins will do very well. The basic recipe:

> one scant cup of granulated sugar
> 3 Tbsp. of liquid (water, milk, or light cream
> 1 Tbsp. butter
> Few drops each of flavoring or extract
> Food coloring as desired

Fruity borstplaat: In a small, heavy saucepan, stir sugar and liquid to a paste. Heat slowly to boiling and cook on low heat without stirring until syrup spins a thread or registers 240° on the candy thermomerter. Remove from heat at once, add the butter and a few drops of fruit extract and coloring. Stir vigorously until the mixture thickens and begins to make a scratchy sound. Drop from tip of spoon onto waxed paper or pour into a greased lid up to ⅓" high. Cool to solidify. Removes easily.

Coffee borstplaat: For the liquid use 1½ Tbsp. cream and 1½ Tbsp. strong coffee. No other flavor is needed.

Chocolate borstplaat: Add 2 Tbsp. of cocoa to the sugar, mix with 3 Tbsp. cream and stir to eliminate lumps before heating.

Mieke's note:
The three foregoing are traditional St. Nicholas recipes. They are courtesy of the booklet "Santa Claus The Dutch Way" published by the Netherlands National Tourist Office.

INDONESIAN DISHES
(INDISCHE SCHOTELS)

For many years, until its independence on December 27, 1949, the Netherlands East Indies were a sizeable island group subject to the Dutch crown, staffed by officers, government ministers and administrative executives. As a result, many of the Eastern dishes became a part of Netherlands cooking. Principally, the succulent and spicy fare known as *rysttafel* is a must for inclusion in any collection of Dutch recipes.

Most if not all cities in Holland feature a number of restaurants where this hearty and varied collection of dishes and accompaniment of sauces are the mainstay of the menu. Specialties of the house will vary according to the chef or the influence of geography itself; i.e. whether the spice and taste leanings are toward Borneo, Java, or Sumatra, to name three of the main islands.

Rysttafel, literally translated to mean "rice table" is perhaps the greatest of misnomers in culinary circles, for it may comprise as many as 30 delicacies in main courses and side dishes, from sweet to salty, delicately bland to torrid, syrupy to granular.

The 2 favorite and basic specialties are *nasi goreng* and *bahmi goreng*. The first uses long grain rice as a base, the second uses a flat noodle in either a rice or wheat grain (*Mie* is the rice flour, *mihoen* the wheat). Accompanying condiments are varied bowls of peanuts, bananas, coconut, beans, onions, jellied sauces, bean sprouts, and many more. *Kroepoek*, a fried shrimp cake, is served hot, and bits of cucumber are to cool one's palate. The sauces include *atjar rampoer* (a relish), *ketjap manis* (sweet soya sauce) and *ketjap asin* (a salty soya), *sambal oelek* (a very hot red pepper sauce) and *Santen*, derived from coconut juice. Other seasonings include *djinten*, *trassi* sticks, *sesateh* and *ketumbar*, all of which are exported from Holland by Conimex Company and readily obtainable in most oriental groceries, gourmet stores and culinary specialty shops.

As for the recipes, I have tried to list all the standards, given to me for use in this book by friends who were born in the Islands.

Nasi Goreng	Gado gado
Soto	Sambal goreng udang
Frikadellen	Kroepoek (Krupuk)
Sateh and Satehsauce	Bami

NASI GORENG

4 cups rice
½ lb. bacon
1 bag *bumbu nasi goreng*
2 large onions—chopped fine
2 tbsps. djinten
2 tbsps. *ketumbar*
2 tbsps. *bumbu sasateh*
1 tbsp. *sambal oelek*
2 cloves garlic—crushed
¼-inch slice *trassi*
1 bunch scallions—cut fine
4 eggs
cooked ham; leftover meat or chicken

Cook rice until nice and dry. Let cool.

Take the *bumbu nasi goreng* and put this in a small dish and cover with enough boiling water so it is well covered. Set aside. Now, cut up the bacon and fry this until crisp in Chinese *wok*. Remove bacon from *wok*, leaving the drippings in. Mix the finely chopped onions with remaining spices and garlic and trassi. Mix real well. Sauté onion mixture in bacon dripping until onions are soft and golden. Now add the *bambu nassi goreng* from small dish and fry another couple of minutes until all is well mixed. Add cut-up ham, meat or chicken to this and mix well again. Now, add cooked and cooled rice and mix thoroughly. Keep frying this rice mixture for 5-10 minutes, then turn heat very low to keep hot, stirring occasionally.

Cut up your scallions, leaving as much of the green as possible. Mix this through the fried rice. Take four eggs, mix with salt, pepper and some bumbu *sasateh* (½ tsp.). Beat the eggs out of pan and cut into thin strips. When the fried rice is thoroughly hot, put on platter and decorate with strips of omelette, and the crisp bits of bacon. Serves 8-10 people.

I always serve pieces of cucumber and an ice-cold glass of beer with this dinner!

Mieke's Note: This original adaptation of this special Javanese dish was given to me by its creator, Ms. Toni Vos of Wilton, Connecticut. I have her permission to use it in this book.

SOTO
(INDONESIAN HOT BROTH)
2 good-sized onions, chopped fine
3-4 tbsps. butter
1 garlic clove, mashed
1 cup finely ground almonds
4 cups chicken stock (broth or bouillon)
pinch turmeric for each serving

In saucepan, sauté the onions, garlic and almonds. Stir in the chicken broth and heat until piping hot. Do not boil through. Serve at once, adding white pepper to taste. Tastes best in a large cup or mug, and may be served with *kroepoek* on the side.

FRIKADELLEN

These can be made in a variety of 3 ways: crab, shrimp, or veal, depending on what you plan around them. Shrimp is most traditional.

1 lb. lean ground veal
        or
lb. crabmeat, canned or fresh, but carefully
        picked over
        or
1 lb. cooked shrimp, ground through food chopper
½ cup breadcrumbs
broth or stock to moisten
knifepoint each of salt, pepper, mace (salt
        may be omitted)
1 egg, separated
1 cup oil in *wok* or iron skillet
½ lb. sautéed mushrooms
½ cup minced parsley
½ cup cream for sauce

In a bowl, mix the meat (or fish) with the crumbs, egg yolk, broth and seasonings. In another bowl, beat egg white stiff and add to the mixture. Heat oil in the *wok* and meanwhile roll small, firm balls between palms of your hands. Cook in the oil, turning gently until they are browned. In separate pan, add the parsley and cream to the mushrooms and pour over the *frikadellen*. Sauce may be omitted entirely if the *frikadellen* are served as an appetizer.

Mieke's note: These recipes come from the collection of Rita Waterman of South Weymouth, Massachusetts. She was born in Soerabaya, Java, and lived there much of her life.

SATEH AND SATEHSAUCE

2-2½ lbs. pork tenderloin (very lean)
1 onion (medium size)
1 clove garlic—crushed
2 tsps. *bumbu sesateh*
2 tsp. *sambal oelek*
3/4 cup *ketjap manis* (Indonesian soya sauce)
¼ cup water
1 tbsp. soya sauce

Mix chopped onion with the spices and the *ketjap*, water and soya sauce. Cut meat into small cubes and put into marinade. Mix very well and let sit for at least four hours, or overnight. Put meat on skewers, four pieces per skewer, and grill over charcoal fire or under grill in the oven. This does not take long as the meat is very tender due to marinating. Use leftover marinade for the *sateh* sauce, which consists of the following:

½ jar gado gado sauce
¼ cup peanut butter, smooth
1 tsp. *sambal oelek*

Mix the above ingredients and the leftover marinade in a double boiler. Heat this, adding water until sauce has required thickness (like thick honey). Serve this piping hot with the grilled *sateh*. These dishes serve 8-10 people.

Mieke's Note: This original adaptation of the Indonesian pork recipe was given to me for use in this book by Toni Vos of Wilton, Connecticut. Born in Pontianak, Borneo, she lived also on Sumatra and Java, and is, needless to say, an expert authority on the varied cuisine of the Islands.

GADO GADO
(COLD INDONESIAN VEGETABLE SALAD)

1 small head cabbage, shredded
1 cup bean sprouts (canned and chopped)
1 cup cooked carrots (cut julienne strips)
1 cup Frenched green beans
2 handfuls raw spinach, well washed
2 cucumbers, slivered
4 shallots or 2 medium onions
2 cloves garlic, mashed
1 tsp. salt
4 chili peppers, mashed
4 tbsps. butter
½ lb. peanut butter
1 cup coconut milk
2 tomatoes, chopped
4 tsps. brown sugar

Be sure all vegetables are thoroughly chilled (including cooked). In medium-size skillet, melt butter and fry together the garlic, chili peppers, shallots. Now add the salt, tomato, coconut milk, tomatoes and sugar. Stir well. Put in a bowl to chill. In large salad bowl, arrange cold vegetables in layers and pour the cold sauce over. May be chilled for an hour before serving. Will serve about 10-12 and is great for a hot summer day's gathering.

Mieke's Note: This recipe is from Carla Massel van Dyk. She was born in Palembang, Sumatra, and now lives in San Francisco, California.

KROEPOEK (also spelled KRUPUK)

These crunchy shrimp cakes were mixed and pounded by hand in the Indies. Now they are available packaged and need only a minimum of preparation.

Heat about 2 cups oil in a *wok* or deep skillet. Heat thoroughly but do not let it smoke, as then the Kroepoek will get too brown. Put 6 to 8 cakes in at a time and turn in about half a minute. Take out immediately when they puff up, and drain off excess oil on brown paper. The recipe calls for a salt sprinkle, but my family finds the shrimp salty enough in itself. These are served with *or bami goreng* and an ice-cold drink.

BAMI

2 lbs. shrimp, cooked and peeled and clean
2 cups cooked pork, cubed or cut in thin strips
1 young green cabbage, chopped
4 medium onions, sliced thin
4 stalks celery, diced
2 cloves garlic, mashed
½ stick butter or margarine (4 tbsps.)
¼ tsp. each ginger, tamarind or tumeric

In a *wok* or iron skillet, melt butter and stir in the cabbage, celery, onions and garlic. Let simmer for about 10 minutes until medium tender (do not overcook). Add the shrimp and pork and heat thoroughly. Serve on a bed of *mie* (*kluski* noodles are the closest if you can't get a package of *mie*.)

Mieke's Note: The above recipes came to me in a roundabout way via my good friend Tuschka Chapman of Miami, Florida. She is a native-born Indonesian. The recipes are from Djakarta.

SAMBBAL GORENG UDANG

2 lbs. raw shrimp, peeled and deveined
large garlic clove, crushed
3 red chili peppers, chopped
2 onions, sliced
large tomato, ripe and peeled
1 rounded tsp. sugar
2 cups coconut milk (2 cups water and 2 tbsps.
   coconut may be substituted)

In a *wok* or iron skillet, mash the tomato and stir in the peppers, onions, garlic and salt. Stir over medium heat and cook until smooth (about 5-6 minutes). Add the coconut milk, sugar, and lastly the shrimp. Cook until shrimp are heated through but still juicy. About 5 minutes should be enough. Keep stirring and do not overcook. Serve piping hot over rice or *kluski* noodles.

Mieke's note: This recipe came to me in a roundabout way from Sarina Saroharto, a native of Bandung...

BEVERAGES
(DRANKEN)

The Netherlands beverage industries are justly famed for their output of *jenever* and malt brews, to say nothing of a variety of mint and cocoa liqueurs. These are often enjoyed as a traditional *borreltje* in late evening. *Advocaat*, preferred by the ladies, is an age-old concoction of egg yolks, cream and cognac, whipped to a thick consistency and eaten with the minutest of spoons.

Certain hot and cold beverages are made at home to celebrate feastdays and special occasions. The ones I remember best are included here.

Bisschopswyn   Boerenmeisjes
Morellen op Brandewyn   Slemp
Boerenjongens   Kandeel

SLEMP
(TRADITIONAL AFTER-SKATING DRINK)
2 qts. whole milk
rind of 1 large lemon, chopped
1 cinnamon stick or ½ tsp. cinnamon
5 whole cloves
pinch of mace
pinch of saffron
pinch of salt
¼ cup sugar
1 rounded tsp. tea or 1 tea bag

Put milk on to boil in saucepan. Tie spices in a cheesecloth bag and drop in milk. Add lemon peel and salt and simmer for 1 hour. Remove spice cachet and serve in large mugs immediately. Mmmmmm.

KANDEEL
(TRADITIONAL BEVERAGE SERVED AT BABY'S BIRTH)
grated peel of ½ lemon
1 cup water
6 egg yolks (save the whites for a soufflé)
about 2 doz. cloves
1 cup sugar
one long cinnamon stick
bottle of white wine, Chablis or Rhine

Tie the cloves and lemon peel in a piece of muslin or cheesecloth. Hang this in small pan with the water and simmer for half an hour. Cool the liquid and reserve. In small bowl, beat egg yolks and sugar. Slowly add the spice liquid and the wine. Boil through gently (in double boiler if you like) and put in jug. Serve with a tall cinnamon stick tied with pink ribbon for a girl, blue for a boy.

BOERENJONGENS—BOERENMEISJES
(A TRADITIONAL FESTIVE LIQUEUR KNOWN AS PEASANT BOYS AND PEASANT GIRLS)
BOERENJONGENS:
1 qt. bottle brandy or cognac
3 cups large white raisins
½ cup brown sugar
cinnamon stick

Place raisins in a saucepan with water to cover. Let come to low simmer and allow to cool until raisins swell up about 2 hours. Drain off excess water and sprinkle brown sugar over. In a large glass jar (preferable wide-mouth and must have a stopper), put the raisins, cinnamon stick and brandy, filling nearly to top. Cover and let stand for three weeks before using. Jar will keep for a year if it isn't all enjoyed by then.

BOERENMEISJES: Same recipe, except we substitute apricots for raisins.

BISSCHOPSWYN
(BISHOP'S WINE) (NEW YEAR'S DAY)
I always suspect that this must be the "smoking bishop" which Scrooge offered to Bob Cratchit at the conclusion of *A Christmas Carol*. It is certainly the Dutch version of it.

2 qts. dry red wine
2 cups sweet vermouth
2 lemons, cored and sliced
3 or 4 small oranges
small handful of whole cloves
few sticks of cinnamon
piece of ginger root or ½ tsp. ground ginger
2 tsps. bitters (optional)

Stud the oranges with the cloves. In an enamel kettle, heat together the wines, fruit and seasonings until *hot* but *not boiling*. Let cool until drinkable and serve in cups or mugs.

Note: This is best when all is mixed the day before and allowed to stand before heating. If served from a tureen, the fruits, etc., may be removed before ladling.

MORELLEN OP BRANDEWYN
(BRANDIED CHERRIES)
2 cups plump red cherries with stems
1 qt. good brandy
cherries should be washed, drained
cut stems so that an inch or so remains
prick 3 to 4 holes in each (leave pits in)

In enamel kettle, heat brandy slightly. Pour in wide-mouth jar, add cherries and seal well. Will keep forever and is best when used a year later. My mother remembers preparing the cherries as a child, and having my grandmother contend that they were best when *overjarig*, i.e. used only after next year's batch was put up. A wide-mouth jar is essential, because the drink is served in a large stemmed glass with a scoop of cherries, which are picked out by their stems.

And oh-so-good with all the above:

KAAS JANTJES
(Cheese Johnnies)
Recipe from Gouda
4 thick bread slices
4 oz. melted butter (1 stick)
grated cheese (fresh is best)

Remove crusts from bread slices and cut into fingers. Dip into melted butter and cover completely with grated cheese. Toast brown on both sides and serve hot with salads or as appetizers. Cheddar or parmesan may be used.

PADDESTOELTJES OP BESCHUIT
(from Alkmaar)
Peel and break in small pieces ¼ lb. mushrooms. Saute in 1 tbsp. of butter and sprinkle with flour, adding cream to thicken. Season with salt and pepper. Place on small rounds or triangles of toast, or bread fried in butter, and top with a small piece of cooked bacon.

Industry
and Export:
DELFT WARE
TILES // SILVER
GOUDA PLATEEL
ARNHEM PEWTER
ZEELAND JEWELRY
LEERDAM CRYSTAL
MAKKUM WARE
DIAMONDS
BARREL ORGANS

ARCHITECTURE VIEWS

TOWERS & TURRETS
COTTAGES & CASTLES
ROOFLINES & GABLES
DIKES & DAMS
CHURCHES & FORTS
FARMS & FACTORIES
GATES & WALLS
and the EUROMAST

"HUTSPOT"

(Another recipe for the traditional dish of the Southern Provinces)

2lbs. beef -- rump or flank (The Dutch call it Klapstuk.)
3 lbs. carrots, sliced
3 lbs. boiling potatoes
3 lbs. sliced onions
3 cups water
1 Tbsp. salt (less may be used)
4 Tbsp. cooking fat (optional)
freshly ground coarse pepper
vinegar for seasoning

Bring the water to a full boil. (Important.) Add salt and meat, and simmer for 2 hours. Now add carrots, cook for 30 minutes more. Potatoes, onions and fat (if used) go in next. Cook until all is well done, adding water if needed. Take out meat with large fork and keep hot. With a coarse masher, mix the vegetables right in the pot. Put them on a hot platter, slice the meat and arrange in slices on top. Sprinkle with plenty of pepper and pass a carafe of good wine vinegar with it. (It tastes even better next day, and that is why the Dutch make it in this large a quantity.)

This casserole is called the "Legacy of Leiden." After 131 days of starvation when the city was under siege by the Spaniards, the Dutch were freed by the Watergeuzen, led by Louis de Boisot, who brought in herring and bread in flat-bottomed barges. Citizen Cornelis Joppenzoon found pots of this Spanish stew outside the city walls, on that memorable day October 3rd. It is eaten every year at that time to commemorate the relief of Leiden.

ROSBIEF GEMARINEERD
(Spiced beef roast from Arnhem)
4 to 5 lb. piece of pot roast
6 large onions, quartered
2 cups each vinegar and water, mixed with
4 bay leaves, 1 tsp. whole cloves, salt and pepper
Margarine or butter for browning

In large bowl, allow roast to marinate in all ingredients for one to three days, turning when you think of it. Pat roast dry, dust with flour and brown on all sides in skillet. Roast in oven for 2-2½ hours, covered, adding the marinade the last half hour. Serve with mashed potatoes or noodles and the jus.

BALKENBREI MET ANANAS
(PINEAPPLE SCRAPPLE)
1 large can pineapple rings, drained and patted dry
4 tomatoes, quartered, dipped in flour and sage
1 lb. piece scrapple, thickly sliced
margarine or butter for browning

Fry pineapple until browned, turning once. Fry scrapple in separate pan. Push to edges and fry tomatoes in the middle. Arrange pineapple and tomatoes around scrapple and sprinkle with more sage.

GLOSSARY OF DUTCH COOKING TERMS IN THIS BOOK

aangemaakt ....mixed
aardappel .... potato
amandel ....almond
ananas .... pineapple
andyvie................................ escarole
asperges .... asparagus
augurken .... pickles
azyn .... vinegar
bain-marie .... water to cover
balkenbrei .... scrapple
bakken .... to fry
bami goreng .... Indonesian dish
blancheren .... to blanch
boerenkool .... kale
bokking .... Holland fish
bot .... flounder
boter ....butter
bruinen........................to brown or sauté
champignons ....mushrooms
chocolade................................ chocolate
court bouillon .... fish stock
deeg ....dough
doperwten .... peas
drogen ....to dry
eend ....duck
eiwit................................ egg white
erwtensoep ....pea soup
frikadellen .... Indonesian deep fry
garnalen .... shrimp
garneren .... garnish
gebak ....pastry
gehakt ....meatloaf
gekruide ....spiced
gelei ....jellied
gemarineerd ....marinated
gember ....ginger
gemengd ....mixed
gerookt ....smoked

91

```
geslagen ............................... whipped
gevulde .......................... filled, stuffed
glazuur ........................... icing, glaze
gratineren .............................to grate
grilleren ..............................to broil
groenten ...........................vegetables
haas ............................ hare or rabbit
hakken ................................to chop
haring ................................ herring
havermout ........................... oatmeal
heilbot ................................fluke
heldere soep ........................clear soup
honing ................................honey
in het zuur ........................... pickled
ingelegd ............................. canned
Jan Hagel ......................... shortbread
jus ............................... pan gravy
kaas ..................................cheese
kabeljauw ...........................codfish
kadetjes ......................... Dutch rolls
kandeel..........................spice beverage
karnemelk ......................... buttermilk
kerrie ................................. curry
kervel ............................... chervil
kip ...................................chicken
kloppen ..............................tò whip
knollen ............................. turnips
koekjes ..............................cookies
koken ................................to cook
komkommer.........................cucumber
kool ................................ cabbage
kreeft ................................ lobster
kroepoek ......................... shrimp cake
kruiden ............................... spices
kropsla ......................... head lettuce
lekker ................................tasty
maizena ........................... cornstarch
mespunt .....................knifepoint measure
moorkoppen..........................creampuffs
nasi goreng ................. Indonesian rice dish
```

oliebollen . . . . carnival doughnuts
ontbyt . . . . breakfast
paling . . . . eel
paneermeel . . . . crumbs
panvet . . . . pangrease
pastei . . . . pastry
peen . . . . winter carrots
pocheren . . . . to poach
poffertjes . . . . *poffertjes*
rabarber . . . . rhubarb
roereiren . . . . scrambled eggs
roeren . . . . to stir
rookworst . . . . sausage
room . . . . cream
roomsoezen . . . . creampuffs
rundvlees . . . . beef
rys ttafel . . . . Indonesian feast
sambal oelek . . . . Indonesian spice
sateh . . . . pork Indonesian
schotel . . . . platter or casserole
schelvis . . . . haddock
seldery . . . . celery
sjalotten . . . . shallots
slagroom . . . . whipped cream
slemp . . . . skating drink
slierasperges . . . . Dutch asparagus
smoren . . . . braising
soto . . . . Indonesian broth
Speculaas . . . . holiday cookies
Stamp pot . . . . casserole dish
stoven . . . . to stew
sudderen . . . . to simmer
tong . . . . sole
uien . . . . onions
uitsmyter . . . . bouncer's snack
varkensvlees . . . . pork
vis . . . . fish
vla (vlaai) . . . . open pie
vlees . . . . meat
vulling . . . . filling

```
Wentelteefjes ........................... bread crêpes
witlof ........................................ .endive
worst ....................................... sausage
wortels ....................................... carrots
```

Windmill language: Each stand of the sails has special significance:

1.) JOY

2.) SORROW

3.) OUT OF ORDER

4.) PRESENTLY OUT OF WORK

5.) REQUEST FOR ASSISTANCE

6.) DECORATED FOR A WEDDING

MEASUREMENT INFORMATION

Household Measurements

3 tsps.	1 tbsp.
5 1/3 tbsps.	1/3 cup
6 tbsps.	3/8 cup
8 tbsps.	½ cup
10 tbsps. plus 2 tsps.	2/3 cup
½ of ¾ cup	6 tbsps.
14 tbsps.	7/8 cup
16 tbsps.	1 cup
2 tbsps.	1 liquid oz.
2 cups	1 pt.
4 cups	1 qt.
2 tsps.	1 dessert spoon
¼ tsp.	1 salt spoon
60 drops	1 tsp.
2 tbsps.	1 coffee measure
28.35 grams	1 oz.
16 oz.	1 lb.

Dry

2 pts.	1 qt.
8 qt.	1 peck
4 pecks	1 bushel
3 bushels	1 sack
12 sacks	1 chaldron

FOR USE IN TRANSLATING FOREIGN RECIPES

1 lb. or 16 oz.	454 grams
A scant *3/4 cup breadcrumbs	100 grams
A scant cup cake flour	100 grams
A scant ½ cup butter	100 grams
A scant ½ cup sugar	100 grams
¼ pound sweet chocolate	1 13 grams
* The measurement given, less 1 tbsp.	

1 kilogram (Kg.)	2.2 lbs.
30 grams	1 oz.
30 centimeters (cc)	1 oz.
1 tsp.	1 dram or 4 cc.
1 tbsp.	appr. 4 drams or ½ oz. or 15 cc.

The above information was invaluable to me in the translation and adaptation of old Dutch recipes. It was compiled by my good friend Maxine Hermansader of West Redding, Connecticut. She is a nutritionist, author of many articles, and one of the world's greatest cooks.

INDEX

TULIPS etcetera -- FACT and FICTION

Legend has it that the tulip was born in Holland! Actually, until 1550 no one in Europe had ever seen one. An Austrian visiting the Turkish sultan found them cultivated in the royal gardens there and brought seeds home.

In 1651, they came to Dutch shores via Switzerland, Germany, and Belgium, and so the Dutch tulip was born. The name originated from its resemblance to a turban, or Tulipan, as it was then called. Holland has since developed hundreds of varieties.

Flowers are a Dutchman's joy. They grace his home, his balconies and windowboxes. They hang from lamp-posts and fountains, gracing all shopping centers with color. Every occasion calls for blooms by the dozens. From tulips to hyacinths, from daffodils to narcissus and croncus, they dot the parks and polders with a blaze of color starting mid-March until late summer, helped by the rich soil and the ever-present rain showers.

Alongside dairy products, bulbs are the prime export of the Netherlands. During the season, armfuls of blooms are for the taking by by visitors. The world's largest open air flower display is the " Keukenhof " (near Lisse), with a second one in " Linnaeushof " (near Haarlem).

Floral pageants and processions dot the calendar year round. Masses of flowers are auctioned daily at Aalsmeer, Hanselersdyk and Rynsburg, using a large clock to cut off the bids.

One of the most important canals in Amsterdam is a floating flower market, and cities of glass are all over the land.

Holland is called, truly, the flower in the lapel of Europe.

WINDMILLS -- Landmark and Legend

A Holland landscape scene almost always depicts a windmill -- and with good reason! Those mills, (both wind and water) have been the friend and mainstay of the Netherlands since the 12th century, and many continue to operate until the present day.

Many of the mills are still privately owned, although some have become historical landmarks and are preserved and maintained by a dedicated society of tradition-minded people.

Each mill is very special and has a name -- religious, whimsical, humorous or historical. Some favorites are: "The Dove," "Four Winds," "Peace," "Our Friend," "The Virgin," "God's Work," "Only Child," "Unity." And then there is the very famous one called "The Rooster" (De Haan) now a restaurant in Amsterdam and dated 1634.

These sails turn into the wind, and sometimes even the entire mill building turns. On windless days, the machinery may be pivoted by horses or donkeys or even electrical power. The mills vary greatly in construction, and depending on size and type, can perform any of the following: cut lumber, grind peanuts into oil, mash grain or mustard seeds, mill flour, and of course pump water from the land to make fields for growing and grazing.

Ten miles north of Amsterdam is a village called De Zaansche Schans. It was the seat of Dutch shipbuilding in 1697 when Peter the Great of Russia came there to study this craft. Five working mills are still open there to visitors, plus the picturesque row of 16 turning mills at "Kinderdyk" (Children's Dike), which is the delight of tourist-photographers.

In all, 1,035 working mills still stand in the Netherlands. National Windmill Day is celebrated annually on May 10th.

Thanks to the windmill, Netherlanders can safely say: "God made the world, but the Dutch made Holland!"

101

BIBLIOGRAPHY

(Sources of Research and Reference)

Encyclopaedia Britannica
Hammond's World Almanac
Holland Herald
Land Of Orange
Molens van Nederland
Aramco World Magazine
Cradle of Colonialism

Mieke wishes to thank also the following for invaluable help, courtesy, and cooperation in supplying data and information, plus even a few of the recipes as noted in the text:

Netherlands National Tourist Office
(New York City) for their publications:

"Welcome to Holland" and
"Santa Claus the Dutch Way."

KLM Public Relations, New York City

The Netherlands Chamber of Commerce

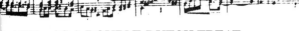

AND...AS A DOUBLE DUTCH TREAT

the MUSIC of the Netherlands!

GREETINGS FROM
HOLLAND
A Product of Monitor Recordings Inc.
Unauthorized Copying Prohibited. Made in U.S.A

Dutch Songs
on **Monitor**
RECORDS

featuring
Mieke and Nina

ON CASSETTE $9.95 ea. ppd.

#51378   (14 songs)   Anywhere in USA

(group and club rates for 10 or more)

A wonderful gift for children of Dutch heritage!

THE DUTCH DOOR ~~BOX 554, SOUTHBURY, CT 06488 U.S.A.~~

Mieke (Pronounced "Mee-ka") was born in New York City of Dutch parents and owes to them her heritage of the food, music and folklore of the Netherlands.

"Holland Cookery" is a four-generation collection of traditional Dutch favorites from all ten provinces, plus a generous sprinkling of colorful anecdotes and historical facts about the Netherlands, its people and its culinary customs.

Because there is simply no other like it, this little book is:

* An invaluable gem for people of Dutch heritage to share ancestral cooking lore with family and friends

* A boon to the epicurean chef

* A real find for cookbook collectors

Book: Cassette:
"Holland Cookery" and   "Greetings from Holland"
are available also through
the catalogue of

ALL THINGS DUTCH
P.O. BOX 419, ACCORD, MASSACHUSETTS 02018-0419
Tel. # 617-340-9500
Fax # 340-9595
OR: 1-800-TRY DUTCH